The Revd Dr Trystan Owain Hugh Cardiff University. He attained an with a thesis on suffering and contemplative prayer, and a PhD in twentieth-century church history from the University of Wales, Bangor. He is the author of *Winds of Change: The Roman Catholic Church and Society in Wales 1916–1962* (University of Wales Press, 1999) and numerous articles (such as two in the prestigious *Journal of Ecclesiastical History*, Cambridge University Press, 2002 and 2005). He runs well-attended meditative retreats and quiet days at parish, diocesan and university level and lectures at Cardiff University and St Michael's College, Llandaff.

FINDING HOPE AND MEANING IN SUFFERING

Trystan Owain Hughes

First published in Great Britain in 2010

Society for Promoting Christian Knowledge
36 Causton Street
London SW1P 4ST
www.spckpublishing.co.uk

British Library Cataloguing-in-Publication Data
A catalogue record for this book is available from the British Library

ISBN 978–0–281–06249–2

Typeset by Graphicraft Ltd, Hong Kong
First printed in Great Britain by Ashford Colour Press
Subsequently digitally printed in Great Britain

Produced on paper from sustainable forests

I dedicate this book to those who have taught me what it means to become as a child to enter the Kingdom of Heaven – especially to my nephews, Aled Siôn, Iwan Rhys, Charlie Llewelyn and Evan Bryn, and my niece and goddaughter, Alis Anwen.

Contents

Acknowledgements

This book has been hewn from both the sharp and the smooth rocks of life experience. As such, I'd like to say *diolch o'r galon* ('thanks from the heart') to everyone who has touched my life over the past 37 years. I especially owe so much to all the people who have stood alongside me during difficult times and to all those who have allowed me to stand alongside them in their own suffering, especially during my curacies in the Rectorial Benefices of Llantwit Major and Whitchurch, Cardiff.

More specifically I would like to thank the following who have directly assisted and supported this book:

Nicola Davies, for her helpful suggestions and continual enthusiasm for the book, despite my asking her to re-read it on far too many occasions.

Kath Lawley, Perry Buck, John and Catryn Rowlands, Peter Jones, Andrew James, Katie Leonard, and Gwynan Hughes, who all gave advice on parts, or all, of the book.

Craig and Ros Bishop, for graciously allowing me to use the email about little Amelia.

Gwydion Thomas for permission to use extracts from R. S. Thomas's poems, the Committee of the Rhys Thomas James Pantyfedwen Lampeter Eisteddfod for permission to use the extract from the hymn 'Pantyfedwen', and Illtud Griffiths for permission to use the extract from J. Henry Griffiths's English translation of the hymn 'Pantyfedwen'.

Acknowledgements

All at SPCK, especially Alison Barr, for believing that others would want to read the book.

The Archbishop of Wales, Barry Morgan, for reading an early draft of the book, and especially for having faith in me when life took unexpected turns.

Kath and Mike Lawley, for their love and kindness during both joyous and difficult times.

Granddad Don Bathgate, for his wise thoughts about 'memories'.

Uncle Llew, Grandma Olive, Nicholas Woodhead, Nain, and Taid, who are all still 'presente'.

My mum (Ros), dad (Berw), and the rest of the family for their continual support and love.

Prologue: beyond thinking

'When things aren't going well during a match, I look at myself'
Cristiano Ronaldo, footballer

'When we are no longer able to change a situation, we are challenged
to change ourselves'
Viktor Frankl

Recently, while tidying areas of my study that had not seen daylight
for many a year, I found a small, yellowed piece of paper. On that
paper was a list I had made as a student of my 'all-time favourite
songs'. It is, of course, only as students that we find the time to
embark on such pointless exercises! But what struck me as I read
that list was that the songs were all thoroughly depressing. They
included such melancholic classics as 'Rainy Days and Mondays',
'I Just Can't Be Happy Today' and 'Heaven Knows I'm Miserable
Now', as well as songs from such dark songwriters as Johnny Cash,
Jacques Brel and Leonard Cohen. Topping the list, however, was
Gilbert O'Sullivan's 'Alone Again, Naturally'. This upbeat song,
in which the singer revels in his pain and his fleeting thoughts
of suicide, joyously asks why God, if indeed he does exist, has
finally deserted him to a life of loneliness and misery.

In reflecting on my list of gloomy songs, it dawned on me that,
as a student, I revelled and dwelt on any misery that came my
way. This was not continual or constant, by any means, as I was
often happy, upbeat, and cheerful. But once there was a chink in
the dam of my emotions, I'd happily allow that dam to collapse.
Melancholy begat melancholy, depression begat depression, and
suffering begat suffering. Worse still, I cultivated an almost perverse
sense of pride in how bad I was seen to be suffering. I even enjoyed
hearing the question 'Can it get any worse for you?'

In November 2006, my life was to change beyond description,
when, at the age of 34, I was diagnosed with a degenerative spinal

condition. The one quality that is widely regarded as determining a person's happiness and fulfilment is health. By all accounts, my back condition, which (after an operation and months in hospital) has left me unable to sit or stand for any length of time, should have, therefore, brought unhappiness. Yet, despite continuing chronic pain, frustration and disability, my illness has actually done the opposite, giving me the opportunity to reflect on where meaning and hope can be sought in our pain and suffering, and then to apply the fruits of this reflection to my day-to-day life.

My story, of course, is in no way unique. One of the first things that struck me when I began my ministerial pastoral work was the fact that behind the smiles of even the most joyous people were, or had been, times of awful suffering and pain. There certainly comes a time in most of our lives when we are forced to take a step back from the everyday existence that we have thus far taken for granted. Such moments can come through illness (either of oneself or of a family member), emotional ill-health, the loss of a loved one, the break-up of a relationship, the loss of a job, or other painful adversities. 'If you look closely enough,' muses Anthony Hopkins as he studies an egg in the film *Fracture* (2007), 'you'll find everything has a weak-spot where it can break sooner or later.' When confronted with our own time of suffering, we are faced with two pathways. We can, of course, allow our struggles to overwhelm us. The Mexican artist Frida Kahlo was blessed with a wonderful talent, but was blighted through her life with misfortune and pain. A tragic road accident as a teenager left her in chronic pain, reliant on opiates and suffering bouts of depression. A turbulent marriage to her fellow-artist and serial womanizer Diego Rivera made matters all the worse. After many years of struggle and pain, she wrote that her suffering was too much to bear and she would never want to return to participate again in this mortal coil.

Other people, however, choose a very different path in their journey through life's vale of tears. They choose to grasp what little joy, hope or meaning life brings, in spite of the most horrific suffering. Viktor Frankl was a prominent Jewish psychiatrist in Austria in the 1930s. His comfortable life was brought to an abrupt end when he was taken to a Nazi concentration camp. He lost all his family there, as his father, mother, brother and his wife were all killed in the gas chambers. He lost his identity there, when he was given 'number 119,104' as a new name. And he and his fellow prisoners were forced to endure the most unimaginable suffering – extreme hunger, cold, violence, and the constant expectation of their own extermination.

> We looked like skeletons disguised with skin and rags, we could watch our bodies beginning to devour themselves . . . one after another the members of the little community in our hut died . . . 'He won't last long', or, 'This is the next one', we whispered to each other, and when, during our daily search for lice, we saw our own naked bodies in the evening, we thought alike: This body here, my body, is really a corpse already.

Yet, even during this time of despair and darkness, Frankl refused to let those outside circumstances quench his enthusiasm for life. 'It is possible to practise the art of living even in a concentration camp,' he wrote, 'although suffering is omnipresent.'

Frankl's experience, along with the experience of others who suffer in diverse ways, are testimony that life *can* hold meaning and hope, even under the most miserable conditions. Our lives, after all, are viewed through whichever lenses we decide to wear. We are the ones who decide how we react to the situations we face. We can see ourselves as blessed, even in the midst of dreadful suffering. Conversely, we can see ourselves as cursed, even if we are living comparatively comfortable lives. It is important that we recognize the timeless truth that each of us has the option to create and cultivate our own world, instead of succumbing to the one that is weighing us down.

By viewing our pain and suffering in a different way, then, we are able to free ourselves from the prisons of our own thoughts and to find hope and meaning in seemingly hopeless situations. Our own minds, after all, contribute so much to our suffering. How we respond to external situations affects our whole being and even the outcome of specific events. Furthermore, many of us are held captive by what can be described as 'screen-saver thoughts'. Like a screen-saver on a computer, we keep returning to certain default thoughts of anxiety and worry, which are individual and unique to each one of us. Our desperate need is to liberate our minds from such incarceration. 'Gonna change my way of thinking,' sang Bob Dylan during his brief flirtation with Christianity. As meaning and hope are food for our souls, it is only by changing our outlook on the world that we will find the internal peace and the external meaning that are necessary for our survival.

Changing our way of thinking, however, will certainly not be an easy journey. The process, which is often long and painful, can be compared to the repentance that John the Baptist preached in the Gospels. The Greek word for repentance (*metanoia*), after all, can be interpreted more literally to denote 'changing one's mind', in the sense of embracing thoughts beyond our present limitations. This book will hopefully set you on your way with this process. Our thoughts, after all, are not us. As Daniel Auteuil maintained in the film *Jean de Florette* (1987): 'It's not me that's crying, it's my eyes.' We are, therefore, able to choose a different way of thinking, and subsequently choose a different past, present and future.

Our journey of change can even be embarked upon in the face of initial reluctance within our hearts and emotions. *Feeling* need not come first, as *doing* can actually lead to new ways of thinking, and that will subsequently lead to a transformation of emotions. In other words, we can, through our minds, make ourselves feel things. There is, after all, a thin line between pretending to feel something and actually feeling something. It is, then, possible to practise the techniques in this book, and its ways of viewing the world around us, before we fully appreciate its underlying philosophy of hope and meaning. Prayer and meditation can, likewise, assist in this process. Frankl notes that it was not those who had a robust nature who coped with life at Auschwitz best, but rather those who developed a sense of spirituality. He puts this down to their ability to 'retreat from their terrible surroundings to life of inner riches and spiritual freedom'. In reflecting on some of the themes presented in the pages that follow, I hope you will recognize that God is not at the end of your journey.

In a sense, God is not even *in* the journey. Rather, God *is* the journey you will be taking.

Chapter 1 of this book will set the scene for our journey of transformation by analysing the suffering that forces us to face eternal questions of hope and meaning. Some writers suggest that when suffering involves physical, psychological and social elements it should be termed 'affliction', while others distinguish between suffering and 'pain', which is simply described as the body's protective network. In this book, however, such terms will not be differentiated, and 'pain', 'suffering' and 'affliction' will be used interchangeably to encompass our individual experiences of loss, grief, damage, disablement or hurt. The chapter does not, however, aim to deal with the question of theodicy, as numerous other volumes exhaust the 'problem of pain' (a number of which are listed in the bibliography for this chapter). Rather, the chapter will explore the paradox that learning *how* to suffer and *how* to wait patiently is the secret of finding joy and hope in our lives. **Chapters 2 and 3** will then present the 'foundations' that underlie our journey towards discovering hope and meaning in our everyday lives. By engendering the practice of 'awareness' and 'acceptance' daily, we can allow ourselves to take a step back from our anxieties and worries, and start to appreciate, in the words of singer-songwriter David Gray, 'life in slow motion'. Once these twin-foundations have been laid, they can then be employed to help us build a tower of hope and meaning in our lives. **Chapters 4 to 8** are, therefore, described as 'building blocks', and they consist of an assessment of how, in spite of suffering, God can work through art, nature, memory, laughter, and love of neighbour. After all, when we are in the desert, God gives us manna to eat and springs of refreshing water to quench our thirst.

In a general sense, all the subjects covered in this book are rooted in the biblical tradition, and will be shown to be so. In a more specific sense, however, the 'foundations' and the 'building blocks' will be expressly related both to the Christian contemplative tradition and to Viktor Frankl's *Man's Search for Meaning*. Exploring Frankl's reflection on the horrors of the Holocaust allows us to recognize that if meaning can be discovered in the place that has become a modern personification of suffering, then it can also be found in our own torn and troubled lives. Christian contemplatives and mystics down the ages, on the other hand, have related the hope in our pain and tragedy directly to God's presence. As Julian of Norwich reminded us, we should not obsess about our condition when we suffer, but rather we should turn towards the 'endless delight of God'. By the time we arrive at the close of this book in the **Epilogue**, then, it is my hope that, no matter how overwhelming our present suffering may seem, we might in some way accept that, echoing the words of T. S. Eliot's *Four Quartets*, the only real tragedy is for us to have experienced our lives, but to have failed to grasp the meaning.

1

Suffering

———•◆•———

'Suffering is a fierce, bestial thing, commonplace, uncalled for, natural as air'
    Cesare Pavese, shortly before his suicide at the age of 42

'These times are dark, but every shadow, no matter how deep, is threatened by the morning light'
    Rachel Weisz in The Fountain *(2006)*

Introduction

In the film *Cinema Paradiso* (1988) the character Alfredo voices a sentiment that many of us feel at times in our lives. 'With all due respect to the Lord who made the world in two or three days,' he says, 'I'd have taken a bit longer, but certain things I could have done better.' If we were playing God, there are certainly things about our fallen world that we may well want to change. Even at happy and upbeat times in our own lives, 24-hour news channels serve as a constant reminder that the dark side of life is uncomfortably close. The world continues to be troubled in so many different ways – wars, natural disasters, murder, child abuse, prejudice, hatred and racism. When we personalize suffering, the situation seems even worse, as each one of us has endured pain and suffering at many levels during our lives. We may have lost someone we love, have been affected by illness or disability, have experienced broken relationships, have lost a job, or have experienced other traumas in our lives. Such incidences often take us by surprise, as they strike without warning and with devastating consequences. The playwright Christopher Fry compares the impact of suffering on our lives with an innocent walk on a minefield. 'One minute you're taking a stroll in the sun,' he writes, 'the next your legs and arms are all over the hedge.' He simply concludes that 'there's no dignity in it'.

The presence of such awful and indiscriminate suffering in the world is certainly one of the greatest challenges to belief in a loving God. As misery breaks through and our worlds are turned upside-down, words like 'grace' and 'mercy' often seem defunct. It is, therefore, unsurprising that the unfairness and injustice of life is one of the principal reasons given for rejection of God. In the song 'Dear God', the 1980s group XTC stood alongside many of their fellow agnostics and atheists in positing the depth of pain and misery in the world as a reason for their apostasy. God stands accused of failing his creation, as wars, natural disasters and vicious diseases render him culpable. The song concludes that Father, Son and Holy Ghost are nothing but 'somebody's unholy hoax'.

Christians themselves have long recognized that suffering has the potential to alienate people from the faith. 'If this is the way you treat your friends, it is little wonder you have so few of them,' the sixteenth-century mystic St Teresa of Avila was overheard screaming up at God when her ox-cart overturned. The consequence of suffering is, however, often more wide-reaching than a mere rejection of faith. Many fall into resentfulness, intolerance, callousness or insensitivity as a result of their afflictions. It is certainly not our place to judge those who succumb to such bitterness or hard-heartedness, but each and every one of us does have the option of taking a different path through the dark night of our pain.

In facing our suffering, then, our aim should not be to explain away or justify, in the words of Dostoevsky, 'the human tears with which the earth is soaked from its crust to its centre'. Rather, our aim should be to start to make larger sense of, and ultimately learn through, the apparent senselessness of our circumstances. After all, if we are to find meaning and hope in our lives, then it must be equally valid, if not *more* valid, in times of suffering as it is in times of comfort. Furthermore, at the centre of that search for meaning and hope must be the experience of the world's freely given love. Our world may well be deeply flawed in its present form, but it still offers us a wonderful experience of the love that flows from joyous and life-affirming gifts such as laughter, nature, memories, art and other people. Nietzsche reminded us that 'he who has a *why* to live can bear with almost any *how*'. It is in these gifts, which for Christians could be termed 'glimpses of transcendence' or 'rumours of another world', that we can discover the *why* in our torn and troubled lives.

Learning to view suffering differently

Our individual groans of suffering, however comparatively mild they sometimes seem, must all be recognized as significant. In the film comedy *Blades of Glory* (2007), starring Will Ferrell, a pair of champion figure skaters lament the embarrassment of the entry of an all-male pairing into the World Championships. 'Two men skating together?!' bewails one of them. 'And in our division no less! Why is God singling us out for the greatest suffering the world has ever known?!' While this assertion provides a comedic moment in the film, it does, in fact, stumble across an important truth. Despite the terrible losses and trauma he endured in the death-camps of Poland, Viktor Frankl warns against anyone claiming a monopoly on suffering. Rather, he suggests that *all* suffering should be taken with utmost seriousness, however brief or minor it proves to be. The 'size' of suffering, after all, is relative. It is, he claims, like releasing gas into an empty chamber – it doesn't matter how much gas is released, it will fill the chamber completely. In other words, it does not matter how great or small our sufferings are, they will always hold the potential to darken our hearts completely. It is only natural, then, that we often become self-absorbed, introverted and self-centred during times of suffering. This, in turn, can lead to a crippling guilt or self-hatred.

Rather than dwelling on such unhelpful emotions, however, we need to be rewiring our ways of looking at the world and, therefore, putting our energies into the paradox of forging meaning from the apparent meaningless of our suffering. After all, one thing we have left through any amount of suffering, great or small, is a choice of *how* we react to what we are enduring. 'The nature of rain is the same,' as the Arabian saying reminds us, 'but it makes thorns grow in the marshes and flowers in the garden.' Our choice, then, is twofold – do we lament and give in to our trials and tribulations, or do we embrace life in the midst of suffering? However much it seems that our particular suffering might overwhelm us, embracing life is an option *all* of us are gifted. Contrary to some blinkered claims by science, we are not inescapably influenced by our genes, backgrounds and surroundings. Each of us is more than a mere product of our environment and our conditioning. We *can* decide what becomes of us mentally and spiritually. This is often the only real freedom left to us. It is, therefore, the way we bear suffering that brings meaning to our lives. 'The way in which a man accepts his fate and all the suffering it entails, the way in which he takes up his cross,' writes Frankl, employing Christian imagery, 'gives him ample opportunity – even under the most difficult circumstances – to add a deeper meaning to his life.'

We are not aiming, then, to put an end to our suffering, or even to directly increase our happiness. Rather, we should be endeavouring to think about suffering in a different way and to cope with adversaries better. We are not, after all, called to bear our suffering passively, but instead to embrace a life and love that is bigger than our present trials and tribulations. The feeling that we are powerless to change our situations is a fundamental element in suffering. Yet suffering need not make us powerless. We can proactively make a decision to integrate our manifold forms of suffering into a lifelong journey of learning. By rewiring our thoughts and our attitudes, we can experience the life-affirming richness of our existence, even in the midst of seemingly dehumanizing suffering.

Exploring the problem of theodicy, then, will not bring about personal transformation. What we need is something far more practical and radical. John Donne found that his periods of sharpest suffering were the times when his character and spirituality developed most. A great picture, after all, needs shadows and dark corners, alongside the bright colours and light. By recognizing this fact, pain can be transformed and suffering can be redeemed.

When we accept reality in all its terrible fullness, we can, therefore, start to transform it into something wonderful and life-affirming. After all, the journey to the land of milk and honey began by learning how to flourish in the desert.

Suffering and scripture

Despite the problem of theodicy, or perhaps precisely because of it, Christianity has long taken suffering seriously. Scripture itself bears witness to suffering's central role within the Christian faith.

In the Old Testament, the history of Israel is one of struggle and pain, from the tribulations of the patriarchs, through to slavery in Egypt and exile in Babylon. The Wisdom literature tradition voices questions of justice in this context, as it ponders the necessity and character of our daily struggles, especially in relation to an omnipotent God. The desolation of a good person, for example, is the principal theme of the book of Job. The psalmist, on the other hand, describes the silence of God in times of human adversity. Such biblical passages echo our own contemporary protests of anger and frustration when we feel rejection and pain.

In the New Testament, Christ shows himself to be sensitive to the groans of a suffering world, as he offers healing and solidarity to those in the throes of adversity. Furthermore, the anguish of Gethsemane and the blood and pain of Calvary place suffering very much at the centre of our faith. Mel Gibson's controversial film *The Passion of the Christ* (2004) shockingly brings home to us the gruesome agonies of the Good Friday story. Another film, Martin Scorsese's adaptation of Kazantzakis' *The Last Temptation of Christ* (1988), suggests, quite plausibly, that Christ, who was tempted like us in every way (Heb. 4.15), would have faced one final temptation – to resist the tortured death on the cross. One of God's great victories was, therefore, in overcoming the temptation to become a 'Messiah without the cross' and in accepting the agony of the crucifixion. This, consequently, gives us courage to take up our cross and accept our own suffering.

Yet, extreme interpretations of such biblical material pertaining to suffering have, in the past at least, tended towards self-hatred and masochism. Liturgical prayers of certain traditions have been awash with self-humiliation and insults against humanity, while self-mortification has been regarded by some Christians as a path to holiness and penitence. To 'take up our cross', however, should not mean that we are searching out emotional suffering or celebrating our physical pain. Affliction is not to be revelled in or perversely enjoyed. In the same way, suffering should not be regarded as some test from a fascist God, who demonstrates his greatness by breaking our pride and exploiting our dependency. God does not want us to suffer, and he certainly does not use suffering to punish us or to impart some sort of message to us.

Our faith *does* teach, however, that God meets us in our afflictions, bringing meaning and hope at the most unlikely times. Frankl notes that the people who survived the horrors of Auschwitz were not the physically strong and robust. Rather, those who survived were those who found strength despite, and sometimes through, their suffering. Such an assertion was also made almost two thousand years earlier by St Paul, not a stranger to suffering himself. Paul, who described his own personal torment as his 'thorn in the flesh', suggested to the Church in Corinth that those who are strongest are those who find meaning in the apparent meaninglessness of affliction. 'Three times I pleaded with the Lord to take [my suffering] away from me,' he wrote in 2 Corinthians 12.7–10, 'but he said to me, "My grace is sufficient for you, for my power is made perfect in weakness." For when you are weak, then you are strong.' It is, then, through discovering the presence of God's love in our suffering, that we discover renewed strength, hope and meaning in our lives.

God in our suffering

God, then, does not cause affliction, either directly or indirectly. He is not an executioner, a tyrant, nor even a mere spectator. Rather, he is present in our suffering, helping to redeem and transform it. As the Old Testament shows us, God shares the pains of his beloved sons and daughters, as he suffers alongside the persecuted, imprisoned and victimized. 'In all their distress, he too was distressed,' Isaiah 63.9 tells us. The Jewish belief that God not only shares our misery, but also actually dwells within our suffering (*shekinah*), is found in later Kabbalistic teaching. Such a concept plays out in a vivid and literal manner in the New Testament, as, in the words of theologian Jürgen Moltmann, 'the crucified God' takes on the role of the 'suffering, poor, defenceless Christ'. In the Koran, God rejects the humiliation of suffering and pain, putting a criminal in place of Jesus on the cross. Yet, it has always been paramount for Christians that Christ himself experienced the rejection, torture, and pain of crucifixion and death. As such, God is shown to be no stranger to suffering, and he continues to stand with his children as we take up our own crosses and encounter our own crucifixions. This, then, underlies the paradox that many Christians recount – that when they are stripped bare, when they touch the bottom of the abyss, when they experience death while living, it is then they encounter God in a vivid way. 'If the doors of perception were cleansed,' wrote William Blake, 'everything would appear to man as it is: Infinite.'

Through his presence in our suffering, then, we can grow closer to God. Christ's sorrows on the cross show to us that God truly understands our dark times and that he is, in a very real way, dwelling in the journey of our suffering. The former Dean of Westminster Abbey, Michael Mayne, while dying of throat cancer, recognized the transcendent in the midst of his painful battle. 'The darkness', he wrote, 'will not overwhelm us and do us harm. Yes, I find God in the evil of my cancer. Not that he sent it, but that he is found in it and through it.' Mayne even refers to God's 'dark glory' in his terrible journey to the grave.

The very real presence of God in suffering can certainly stand as a comforting reassurance. Yet, the practical reality is that, to many of us, God seems distant, if not absent, during our times of affliction. Christ's impassioned cry from the cross, taken from Psalm 22, encapsulates our pain and frustration: 'my God, my God, why have you forsaken me?' Those times when the still small voice of calm seems mute may well be frequent for us, but, as we will see in later chapters, there are ways in which we can actively search out and recognize that voice in our suffering. God does not want us to suffer, but, when we do, our misery can lead to spiritual, emotional and mental development. As Simone Weil suggested, the Christian faith offers 'no supernatural remedy for suffering', but it does strive for 'a supernatural use for it'. Like the risen Christ, we will always bear the scars of our suffering, the nail-marks of our own crucifixions, but we can still emerge from our darkness transformed and redeemed. We will not, therefore, have been subject to a cross of meaninglessness, but, rather, we will have learnt to affirm life by equating our suffering with the cross of Christ and its promise of resurrection.

God in our waiting

When we suffer, then, we should remember that we are participating in the three days of the cross (the *triduum*). By doing so, we accept the reality and pain of our own Good Friday, we dwell in the frustrations and darkness of Holy Saturday, and we search for those life-affirming glimpses of resurrection and hope of Easter Sunday. Many people who suffer, however, remain stranded in the darkness of Holy Saturday, and fail to recognize that such a time of waiting, however frustrating, is where resurrection is birthed. In the film adaptation of Jane Austen's *Mansfield Park* (1999), Sir Thomas Bertram falls gravely ill. His son Edmund gingerly asks whether anything can be done. 'Wait,' comes the answer; 'for time can do almost anything.' Yet, in our fast-food, microwave-meal world, waiting is seen as having little or no value. It so often seems like a frustrating waste of time. After all, we are taught from an early age that waiting constitutes 'dead time' that eats into our busy, constructive days. During any 'dead time' that we face, we feel we can always be doing something more interesting, something more worthwhile. As we juggle our busy schedules, the phrase 'multi-tasking' has even become a badge of honour to be worn proudly in the overflow of our lives. We will, indeed, do anything to avoid 'wasting' time.

In the context of suffering, the frustration of waiting is intensified – waiting for recovery from illness, waiting for depression to lift, waiting for light to break through grief, waiting for test results, or waiting for the hurt of broken relationships to heal. We often, therefore, fail to recognize that so-called 'dead time' can actually be a time for great spiritual and personal growth. At the end of A. A. Milne's *House at Pooh Corner*, Christopher Robin 'grows up' by leaving his childhood toys and childlike ways behind:

'Pooh,' he announces to his little bear, 'I'm not going to do Nothing no more.'

'Never again?' asks Pooh.

'Well, not so much,' comes the answer, 'they don't let you.'

There is something profoundly true about that sentiment. Rarely as adults do people allow us just to do 'nothing'; rarely do people allow us just to 'be'. We live, after all, in a culture of 'doing', rather than 'being'. Thus, achievements have become our yardstick to success and growth, while doing 'nothing' is frowned upon.

Life, growth and movement are, then, inextricably linked in today's hectic world. The journalist Herb Coen considered the gazelles and the lions on the plains of Africa. Every morning the gazelle wakes up and knows it has to run faster than the fastest lion or it will be killed. Every morning the lion wakes up and knows it has to run faster than the slowest gazelle or it will starve to death. So, Coen claims, whether we are lions or gazelles, when the sun comes up, we'd better be running. Our modern lifestyles certainly teach us that running is what life is really about; that life is about doing, achieving, competing, and winning. Little wonder that pharmacological and therapeutic treatments for stress, depression and anxiety disorders are costing our National Health Service in excess of £9 billion per year in England alone.

While there is certainly much running for survival in the natural world, Coen's anecdote holds merely a partial truth. Most strikingly, it fails to recognize that rest and play, not activity, are often at the heart of the animal kingdom. Lions and gazelles certainly run when they need to, but most of their lives are spent lazing around, playing among themselves, or, in the case of the gazelles, grazing on the plains. In a sense, *that's* what we need to recover. We need to recover time to stop and stare. Time to be still. Time to listen. Time to appreciate the joys of life, however fleeting they seem during our suffering. Time just to 'be'. The oft-inebriated actor Richard Harris is said to have been asked by a policeman why he was lying in the middle of a street in London at three in the morning. 'Well,' came his apocryphal answer, 'I've heard the world spins around, so I thought if I stay here long enough my house will go past.' During difficult periods of our lives, we too need to take time just to stop and let the world spin around us. After all, growth still happens when we're doing nothing – growth happens in our times of darkness, growth happens in our times of silence, growth happens in our times of waiting.

Waiting, then, affords us the opportunity just to stop and stare, and, if we are willing to search for them, that will provide moments, however brief, when God will break through and touch us. Winters can certainly be long, cold and painful, but signs of spring will always burst forth. The apophatic paradox is that God's presence can even be sensed in his seeming absence. 'As I had always known,' Welsh poet R. S. Thomas wrote, 'He would come, unannounced, remarkable merely for the absence of clamour.' However dark and long our Holy Saturday seems, and however deep the nails of suffering have pierced our palms, we *can* find God, if only we first know where to search. 'I will take refuge in the shadow of your wings,' announces Psalm 57, 'until this time of trouble has passed.'

Suffering and love

This concept of growth through the long wait of our suffering is, of course, not specifically Christian. Other world religions, contemporary psychology and secular culture in general recognize that meaning, formation and development can be forged through trials and troubles. 'It's only when you've been in the deepest valley,' mused Anthony Hopkins in his role as Richard Nixon in the film *Nixon*, 'will you ever know how magnificent it is to be on the highest mountain.' The uniqueness of the Christian response to suffering is, however, found in the centrality of God's grace. As such, we are faced with yet another paradox. The tears and tragedy of the cross are a sign of God's love for us precisely *because* they guarantee his loving presence in our own tears and tragedies. God is love, and just a glimpse of that love can powerfully illuminate the darkness that we are going through. 'And here in dust and dirt, O here,' wrote George Herbert, 'The lilies of His love appear.' We can, then, aim to draw closer to God's love in the midst of our suffering. Pain may well remind us that we are alive, but love reminds us *why* we are alive. Thus, we need to retrain our minds to recognize those times in our daily lives when God's light breaks through our darkness – times we hitherto have taken for granted or ignored. These moments have a cumulative ability to transform, illuminate, and bring us hope. Held as a hostage for many years in a dark room in Beirut, Brian Keenan recalls how he made a candle from small pieces of wax and string from his clothing fibres. 'Quietly, calmly, a sense of victory welled up in me,' he later wrote, 'and I thought to myself without saying it, "They haven't beat us yet. We can blot out even their darkness."' Light, of course, does not avoid darkness. Rather, it confronts it head on. 'The light shines in the darkness,' asserts the Gospel of John 1.5, 'but the darkness has not understood it.' Likewise, love's concern is not the avoidance of suffering, but rather its transformation, as our painful experiences become productive and strengthen us.

Jesus certainly knew that the existence of evil and suffering was a mystery to humankind. He would have been well acquainted with the book of Job and with the psalms of sorrow, and he stood before his people as the suffering servant of Isaiah. Yet, he himself was more concerned to proclaim the mystery of *love* than give hollow platitudes about the mystery of suffering. Love, like suffering, cannot truly be explained. It can, however, be experienced. We will now, therefore, go on to explore how we can experience God's love in the midst of our pains. Dostoevsky suggested that every creature knows its purpose in life – from the bees in the beehive, to the ants in the anthill. 'Only humankind does not know its formula,' he concludes. We will now explore how the everyday practice of awareness and acceptance can help us to discern that formula in our own turbulent lives.

2

Foundations: awareness

'We are not human beings having a spiritual experience, we are
spiritual beings having a human experience'

Pierre Teilhard de Chardin

'Vermeer: "Look at the clouds – what colour are they?" Griet: "White.
No, not white. Yellow. Blue. And grey. There are colours in the
clouds!"'

Colin Firth and Scarlett Johansson in Girl with
a Pearl Earring *(2003)*

Introduction

There is an old Eastern tale, about a little fish in the ocean, that
sheds light on the question of where God is to be found. The
inquisitive fish asks a passing dolphin, 'Excuse me, sir, where can
I find the thing they call the ocean?' The dolphin answers, 'Well,
the ocean is what you're swimming in.' 'This?' the little fish
says, 'No, this is water! I'm looking for the ocean.' He swims away
disappointed, still searching for that elusive ocean. Many of us
find ourselves in a similar situation in our quest for the divine.
So determined are we to discover something spectacularly supernatural, that we fail to recognize God's majesty and grace all
around us. The transcendent, after all, resides in life's details.
He is present in the people we meet, in the beauty of nature, in
the bliss of silence, in the comfort of our memories, and in the
joy of laughter. In fact, if we are tuned to love's frequency, we
can find God in most of our seemingly ordinary and everyday
experiences.

Dwelling in the present moment

Acknowledging the theoretical presence of God in the world is certainly very different from becoming truly 'aware' of the transcendent all around us. For us to find meaning and hope in our lives, both outside and within our suffering, we need to develop an awareness that allows us to experience God as naturally as we breathe the air around us. In the Gospels, Jesus commands his disciples to announce to the world that 'the Kingdom of God is near'. The Greek word for 'is near' (or 'at hand') can, however, be translated back into Hebrew or Aramaic to give the meaning 'is here'. According to this fresh perspective, Jesus affirms the Kingdom of God as a present reality. In other words, an experience of God is not to be some distant dream for our futures, but is something for us to discover *now*, in our everyday lives. This is the 'sacrament of the present moment', as described by the eighteenth-century monastic Jean Pierre de Caussade, where we come into contact with the transcendent in the here-and-now, in our everyday experiences.

While the centrality of the present moment in Buddhist mindfulness meditation is unambiguous, its historical prominence in Christian traditions is less recognized. Yet, from as early as the fourth-century desert fathers of Egypt, the contemplative tradition has acknowledged the power of the here-and-now. Historically, this has differed fundamentally from Buddhism in its insistence that God himself resides in that moment. By today, contemplative prayer is not a monastic peculiarity, but has become an integral part of most mainstream denominations.

For us to practise such an awareness of God in the here-and-now, however, is certainly not straightforward. While we experience God in all sorts of wondrous ways, our minds tend to process these encounters and put labels on our experiences. Imagine walking in a park one dark evening and noticing a flash of wonderful colour and light in the distance. For a moment our breath is taken away by its sheer beauty, but then, as the speed of sound catches up with the speed of light, we hear an accompanying explosion. Naturally, our minds immediately label this as a 'firework' and we remember that this is Bonfire Night. Before we know it, rather than savouring a moment of transcendence, we begin thinking about how quickly Christmas is coming around or how we must remember to pick up food for our own bonfire party. All too often, then, our own thoughts alienate us from the transcendence of each moment. Instead, we create a running commentary in our minds, continually rerunning the past and scripting the future.

We need, therefore, to learn to capture and savour that awareness of awe and wonder for the here-and-now, which our own minds so often unwittingly work to destroy. In this sense, some non-Christians can 'experience' God in a fuller way than do some devout Christians, even though they might not label their experiences as spiritual. Anyone who is able to connect with the present moment is, after all, naturally drawn into the divine. This often happens through interests and hobbies that allow powerful experiences of the here-and-now – cooking, gardening, nature, hiking, music, film, art, theatre, and so on. What is unique about being Christian, though, is that when we connect with the present moment in such a way we can recognize it for what it truly is – a loving experience of the Kingdom of God.

Dwelling in the past and the future

The twenty-first-century lifestyle is one of convenience and haste. 'I put my instant coffee in my microwave oven and almost went back in time,' quipped the American comedian Steve Wright. Most of us struggle to divide our already busy lives to include everything that experts tell us we should be doing – exercising, socializing, working, eating well, sleeping, spending time with family, and so on. Sometimes our lives seem to whiz by so fast that we would give anything for a remote control that could rewind or pause time. At other times we feel so unhappy or anxious that, like Adam Sandler in the film *Click* (2006), we would find a fast-forward button far more useful. Yet for us to truly discover meaning and hope in our lives, we need to search out and appreciate God's love in the present reality of each and every moment of our lives, however difficult that will often be.

Instead of appreciating and savouring the present moment, however, our hectic and demanding lives lead us to grasp ever more tightly and jealously the thoughts that are unconsciously firing through our minds. These are often thoughts about our past, as we relive former glories, wallow in regret and bask in nostalgia. By comparing the moment-to-moment passing of our lives with the viewing of a film, we are able to see something of the danger of spending too much time dwelling in the past. Our enjoyment of a film, after all, lies in our readiness to appreciate scenes and then let them pass. If we enjoy one scene in particular, we do not keep rewinding that scene and watching it over and over again. However comforting or exciting the scene might be for us, by continually replaying it we actually cease to be watching a 'film'. Similarly, our minds can end up playing the same scenes from our past over and over again. Thus, we are not *truly* living any more, but, rather, dwelling in a false reality.

Our minds, of course, are also filled with thoughts about the future. We make plans, we look forward with anticipation, and we worry about impending events. Living in the future, however, will often lead us to become stressed, anxious and depressed. It can also result in us living in a fantasy world of expectation that engenders a constant stream of anti-climax. 'So, are you looking forward to the big disappointment?' a friend revealingly asked a month before one Christmas. There certainly *is* something anti-climactic about anything we spend so long looking forward to. Yet, our consumer society teaches us to live our lives in the future – Christmas gets sold to us in August, the January sales start on Christmas Eve, and the Easter eggs are on the shop's shelves even before January closes. For many of us, life has become something that happens *to* us while we are busy anticipating or dreading our futures.

We need, therefore, to train our minds to move away from dwelling in the past or in the future. 'Fear not for the future, weep not for the past,' wrote the poet Shelley. After all, it is only in the present moment that, paradoxically, we will find the strength to transform both our pasts and our futures. The here-and-now is, after all, holy ground, where God is met and lives are changed. A popular saying maintains that 'the past is history, the future is mystery, but the present is a gift – that's why it's called the present.' Once we are able truly to appreciate that wonderful gift of the present moment, then God can help us transform both our memories of the past and our worries for the future.

Child-like awe and wonder

Such a rooting in the present moment does, in some way, return us to the sense of wonder and joy at the world that we experienced as children. I remember watching my two-year-old nephew playing in a field. He would pick up a blade of grass and just stare at it with amazement. Then he would hold it up to the sun and watch the sunlight bounce off it. Finally, he'd put it down, then pick a daisy, and the process of awe and wonder would start again. 'I wish I liked anything as much as my kids like bubbles,' muses Paul Rudd in the film *Knocked Up* (2007); 'their smiling faces just point out our inability to enjoy anything.' If the Kingdom of God is 'here', then perhaps this attitude of deep wonder at God's gifts to us is the background to Christ's assertion in Mark 10.15 that we have to become as a child to enter the Kingdom of God.

Aside from our own childhoods, there are certain other times in our lives when we are drawn to appreciating the present moment in all its fullness. Time spent with children, for example, will allow some of us to step outside our usual limitations, as children's sense of marvel can take on an infectious quality. Likewise, the sense of perspective discovered at the end of our lives often allows us to experience things as they really are, not as our thoughts tell us they are. In the book *Tuesdays with Morrie*, a real-life description of one individual's battle with motor neurone disease, Morrie nods towards the window saying:

> You can go out there, outside, any time. You can run up and down the block and go crazy. I can't do that. I can't go out. I can't run. I can't be out there without fear of getting sick. But you know what? I *appreciate* that window more than you do.

Restricted to one room in his house, Morrie would look out of the window each day and notice ever more of the world around him – the change in the trees, the strength of the wind, and so on. Echoing the popular hymn 'Morning Has Broken', he describes himself as being drawn towards things as if he was seeing them for the first time. On numerous occasions during my own pastoral ministry among the sick or dying, I have witnessed individuals attune themselves to a similar new-found appreciation of the little time they have left. At such dark and fearful times in their lives, they become truly uplifted by the view from their window, the laughter of a joke shared, the sound of grandchildren playing in the next room, the memory of a special moment in their lives or the tender care of a nurse or relative.

Most of our lives, however, we fail to grasp such a depth of appreciation for life's present moment. We are, after all, constricted by certain factors. Our busy lifestyles certainly hold us back. One of the few astronauts who has walked on the moon tells of how he looked back at the Earth and stood still, in awe of its beauty. Then, on realizing that he was 'wasting time', he returned to collecting rocks. Our belief that we have to be 'busy' is so entrenched in our psyche that we misjudge our priorities. Like Martha in the Gospel story, our rushed lives mean that we do not even notice that Christ is right in front of us. Our lives are such hectic journeys that we fail to recognize the light of God's grace that illuminates our paths. We need, therefore, to start appreciating the present moment as the Kingdom of God on earth. 'Instead of getting to heaven at last,' wrote Emily Dickinson, 'I am going all along.'

Likewise, we rarely capture that child-like awe and wonder because we have grown to be shackled by words and concepts that impede our connection with people and objects. No longer do we see a wonderful, bright sparkling object in the sky that takes our breath away. Instead, we see 'a star', or, worse still, we see 'Alpha Centauri'. Yet, if we are able to bypass these words and concepts, we can return to see reality in a fresh and amazing way. As Meister Eckhart suggested: 'We don't find God by adding anything to our soul; no – we find God by taking things away.' So, we need to strip away words, concepts, and our busyness, and we need to start experiencing life as if for the first time.

The present moment and suffering

Viktor Frankl suggests that while having a future 'goal' was necessary for survival in Auschwitz, 'living' in the future was detrimental to everyday life. What was necessary, therefore, was for the prisoners to turn thoughts of their present lot not to the future or the past, but to more positive elements of their awful existence. 'By this method,' he concludes, 'I succeeded somehow in rising above the situation, above the sufferings of the moment, and I observed them as if they were already of the past.' In the contemporary Western world, many of us have grown so accustomed to our comfortable lives that we do not believe it possible to find light within our dark moments. Many of us, instead, reach out for pseudo-palliatives that offer escape and distraction – alcohol, drugs, food and sex. As a result, such activities have become overly important in so many people's lives. In *Longtime Companion* (1990), a moving documentary film on the effect of Aids on New York's gay community in the 1980s, a man nurses his lover on his deathbed. The narrator asks a deeply spiritual question: 'What do you think will happen when we die?' The reply comes with no hint of irony: 'We'll get to have sex again.' In some ways, sex and drugs do, indeed, root us in the here-and-now. C. S. Lewis recognized this to be the case, as he described the appreciation of nature and art in the present moment as 'so very like sex'. Our quest for transformation, hope and meaning, however, will never be quenched by such short-lived and escapist pleasures. Distraction, after all, so often leads to destruction. What is required is, rather, a whole new way of looking at the world.

Instead of shutting out the sights and sounds of the world during our pain and suffering, we need to be opening our minds and hearts to let them in. By doing so, we will find ourselves free to truly appreciate the wonderful gifts God has given to us. After all, even deserts are brimming with life for those who take the time and energy to open their eyes and search for its existence. As the Israelites wandered in the wilderness, for example, they spent many years complaining of their lot. By doing so, they failed to truly appreciate the grace all around them – water from the rock, bread from heaven, a flock of quail, and so on.

Again, children can teach us something of how we can find such grace in our times of suffering. Children's hospitals are certainly distressing places to visit, and yet the children there often reflect a life-affirming joy and bravery. This is vividly borne out in an email I received from friends of mine, whose three-year-old was being treated for leukaemia:

> Yesterday, Amelia's Hickman line ('wiggly') fractured. The line goes into Amelia's chest and runs under the skin to a major blood vessel in her neck – it is used to take blood samples and administer some of the chemotherapy drugs. At the hospital the medics cut off the damaged section and grafted a new end onto the remaining section of line. Throughout this procedure Amelia sat patiently on Ros's lap as she was covered with a green surgical gown and watched as the line was cut and repaired. As they were driving home Ros told Amelia that she was the bravest girl in the world to which Amelia replied, 'I am the bravest girl in the world and the happiest girl in the world.'

In our increasingly sanitized and perfection-obsessed world, the whole concept of happiness and joy within suffering is alien to us. Yet, sorrowful minor chords and uplifting major chords complement each other so beautifully in a song or a piece of music. We need, then, to attune our minds and our hearts to life in all its fullness, and to begin to appreciate the wonder within each and every moment, whatever we are enduring at that time.

Beginning the journey

Our first step to experiencing meaning and hope in our suffering, then, is for us to start inhabiting the only space where life is truly experienced – the present moment. We do so by attending to the things that for years we have taken for granted. Most of us are, to borrow an image from philosopher William Irwin Thompson, like flies crawling on the ceiling of the Sistine Chapel, blissfully unaware of the beauty all around us. By living one moment at a time, we can truly experience that beauty, whether we find it in nature, in other people, in art, or in any other place. To facilitate this process, we do not need to follow the mystics and contemplatives into the desert or wilderness. Rather, we simply attend to the present moment wherever we are and whatever we are doing. 'Shut your mouth; open your eyes and ears,' writes C. S. Lewis; 'take in what there is and give no thought to what might have been there or what is somewhere else.'

Yet, most of us, even those of us who are Christian, rarely even recognize God's existence in the physical world, let alone 'practise His presence', in the words of seventeenth-century monastic Brother Lawrence. We need, then, to train our senses to meet God in his world. By doing so, we start to view things afresh and to hear and see things as if for the first time. During the intense period of my own illness, I would venture out for very short daily strolls. On one of those walks, I noticed a certain bud on a certain tree. During the subsequent weeks and months, I watched that small bud grow into a wonderful leaf, before changing colour and falling gently to the floor. Despite having walked past countless trees, I had never before taken the time to stop and truly appreciate the sprouting of a bud and the life of a leaf. This was God at work, and, in spite of my continuing pain, I could not help but celebrate his wonderful, mysterious, and holy gift of life. After all, Psalm 118.24 reminds us that '*this* is the day the LORD has made', not yesterday or tomorrow, so 'let us rejoice and be glad in it'.

By inhabiting the here-and-now and by noticing God break through our everyday lives, then, we become aware. But to begin this journey to awareness, we can start even closer to home. Christian contemplatives have long emphasized the need for self-awareness. To grow in an awareness of ourselves, we need simply to quieten our minds as much as possible, and learn to observe in silence our own thoughts and feelings, as if we were watching a film or reading a book. Most importantly, we should not make any judgements on what we notice. During times of suffering especially, our minds overflow with scattered thoughts and feelings. Therefore, we need to take time out of our busy schedules, just to stop in silence and watch our minds at work, accepting without criticism whatever we view. This allows us to separate ourselves from any pain or suffering we are undergoing. We simply observe our thoughts and feelings as they introduce themselves, then glide away. Like bubbles rising up in water, our thoughts and feelings come and they go. Like clouds in the sky, they keep moving through our restless minds. Such non-judgemental observation can subsequently be taken into our everyday lives. As we embrace our own consciousness, we become truly aware of what we are saying, what we are doing, how we are thinking and what our motives are. It is then only a small step to viewing the whole world around us, including nature, other people and the arts, through the lens of such compassionate awareness. Recently, BBC's *Wildlife on One* programme analysed two groups of scientists who were investigating the intelligence of dolphins. One group, based in a dolphinarium in Hawaii, was training dolphins to jump through hoops, throw frisbees, and even watch underwater television. The second group of scientists was out on the seas, simply observing the behaviour of wild dolphins. They were not trying to train the creatures, or get anything out of them. They were merely observing, and, through doing so, they learnt as much, if not more, about dolphins than the Hawaiian research team. That is a great model of awareness for us. We are not forcing anything to happen or trying to compel a change in our predicaments. We have no further agenda than simply to observe ourselves and everything around us. By doing so, we reside in the present moment and we tread on divine ground. We are, therefore, entering the Kingdom of God and our suffering cannot fail to be transformed. After all, in the words of the Jesuit Anthony de Mello, 'in awareness is healing; in awareness is truth; in awareness is salvation; in awareness is spirituality; in awareness is growth'.

3

Foundations: acceptance

'Morrie, who could no longer dance, swim, bathe, or walk; Morrie, who could no longer answer his own door, dry himself after a shower, or even roll over in bed. How could he be so accepting?'
Mitch Albom, Tuesdays with Morrie

'Not to accept an event which happens in the world is to wish that the world did not exist'
Simone Weil

Introduction

In the film *Blood Diamond* (2006), Leonardo de Caprio plays a restless South African who constantly expresses his desire to leave Sierra Leone, where he is involved in the illegal diamond trade. At the end of the film, the character, after a lifetime of selfishness and self-centredness, lays down his life to save his friends, and by doing so, dies in the very same country from which he was trying to escape. As he bleeds to death, his final words are: 'I'm exactly where I'm supposed to be.' Literature and film frequently suggest that acceptance is at the heart of redemption. However difficult our circumstances, with acceptance as the cornerstone of our temple we will be able to affirm our life's journey, trusting that we grow even through our darkest moments. Thus, a large part of discovering hope and meaning in our lives is through a radical acceptance of our circumstances and situations, as we confidently echo those words in our own lives: 'I'm exactly where I'm supposed to be.'

What acceptance is not

By accepting and affirming our circumstances, our suffering certainly need not overwhelm us. It is, however, important for us to recognize that such 'acceptance' is not some passive submission to hardships. It is not merely putting up with, or tolerating, our suffering. It does not even mean that we submit ourselves to blind fate. Such understandings of suffering could result in a dangerous apathy or even lead to an abandonment of hope. Suffering, and its causes, should always be fought against. After all, being liberated from existing suffering is one of the greatest themes of the Bible, not least in the story of the exodus from Egypt in the Old Testament and in passages such as the Magnificat in the New Testament.

Rather than reflecting passive defeatism, then, the notion of 'acceptance' in this context deals with embracing the reality of situations before any action is taken. If we contract a nasty flu virus, for example, we need to accept that we are ill before we carry out a recovery process of sleep, healthy food and medication. Ironically, it is our unwillingness to accept our present lot that so often prevents the possibility of transformation. Embracing acceptance allows us to face pain, illness, injustice and suffering with courage and, therefore, to work alongside God for change and growth.

Sometimes, however, we might be led to a realization that there is no foreseeable way out of our suffering. During those times, we simply accept that we are called to live with our pain or affliction. 'Sometimes', wrote Frankl, 'man may be required simply to accept fate, to bear his cross.' Yet that process of acceptance in itself can help transform our bleak circumstances to a situation of hope and meaning. We certainly do not have to remain a victim to assent to suffering. Jesus' experiences in Gethsemane and in front of Pontius Pilate do not reveal a weak coward, passively accepting suffering and abuse. Rather, he faced his cup of suffering nobly and with courage and compassion. Through following his path to the cross, we can radically say 'yes' to life and, ultimately, to resurrection.

Illusion of control

Most stress, anxiety and worry in our lives is the result of us feeling that we lack control of specific circumstances and situations. In this sense, we are, in the words of George Bernard Shaw, 'feverish selfish little clouds of ailments complaining that the world will not devote itself to making us happy'. After all, the vast majority of us crave power over our own lives. In my work in higher education over the past decade, both as a personal tutor and then as a chaplain, it has been strikingly clear that the numbers of both female and male students with anorexia, bulimia, and/or issues of self-harm have been on a sharp increase. This comes as little surprise in light of the fact that these disorders are centred around a perceived need for control, in a world where 'being in control' is valued so highly. That very same longing for control is evident in most of our lives, especially in our desire for money, happiness or health. Control is, however, ultimately a myth. Not one of us can ever attain complete control of our lives, not least because we are subject to outside influences, such as the actions of other people.

Nevertheless, when things are going well in our lives, we fall for the illusion that we *are* in control. This makes our periods of suffering, when we seemingly 'lose' control, all the more difficult. 'The more we try to take control of our lives, the more it goes wrong,' the character Alex is warned in the BBC drama *Ashes to Ashes*. This illusion of control is not just a lie. It is, in fact, the ultimate lie, as it fundamentally distorts our view of reality. For so many of us, control becomes our ultimate goal. As a result, we use relationships, jobs, education, sex, money and power to persuade our fragile egos that we can, in some way, be in command of our destinies. We only have to peruse the myriad of women's glossy magazines on the shelves of newsagents to recognize the societal pressure on us to try and control the way we act and the way we look. Yet, our desperate effort to control outcomes damages us in so many ways, as we succumb to anxiety, depression, greed or self-centredness.

The paradox remains that, in fact, hope and meaning come to us only when we relinquish control. After all, it is easier to ride a horse in the direction it is going! We receive power, then, by surrendering control. According to John 12.24, unless a grain of wheat falls to the ground and dies, it cannot live. As those undergoing the 12-step programme of Alcoholics Anonymous know, the first step to acknowledging such a limitation of our control is to place our dependence in the hands of a higher power. Yet, often we even desperately attempt to direct God himself. In the story of Mary and Martha in Luke's Gospel, Martha not only refuses to sit and listen to Jesus, but she also tells Jesus what *he* should be doing. Each week at church, Christians pray 'Thy will be done', yet the rest of the week we tell God exactly how we want him to organize our lives and our situations!

Indeed, in the great card game of life, we are all dealt our hand and we play it to the best of our ability. Unhappiness and hopelessness, however, come when we shout and scream that we should have been dealt a different hand, or, worse still, that we should have been dealt another person's hand. Hope and meaning come when we relinquish our desperation to control the game, and we begin to put our trust and dependence in God as we play our hands of cards. Only then, when we find ourselves tempted to wish for a change in our hands, will we be able to instead ask for God to grant us peace, meaning and hope whether our hands change or not.

God has a plan

Scripture certainly does not minimize hardship, as we see from the story of Job, the passion of Christ and books such as the Psalms and Lamentations. It does, however, suggest that we withhold our judgement about suffering until all the evidence is revealed to us. The eighteenth-century Jesuit Jean Pierre de Caussade suggests that, in the mean time, we abandon ourselves to divine providence. In other words, we must trust that God has a plan, and we must accept and allow that plan to happen. 'What he ordains for us each moment,' he wrote, 'is what is most holy, best, and most divine for us.'

There will be times in our lives, then, when awful things *will* happen to us, to our families and to our friends. God certainly does not want such things to happen. Yet his good purpose can shine through, even in those most terrible moments of life, as Philippians 2.13 attests. However much God despises our suffering, he stands with us in our pain and employs our troubles as part of his bigger plan. In an old Chinese story, a farmer owns a solitary horse that he uses to plough his fields. One day the horse escapes into the hills and the farmer's neighbours sympathize with the old man over his bad luck. The farmer replies, 'Bad luck? Good luck? Who knows?' A week later, the horse returns with a herd of wild horses and so the neighbours congratulate the farmer on his good luck. His reply again is, 'Good luck? Bad luck? Who knows?' When the farmer's son is attempting to tame one of the unruly horses, he falls off and breaks his leg. The neighbours sympathize with the old man over his bad luck. The farmer again replies, 'Bad luck? Good luck? Who knows?' Finally, some weeks later, the army comes to the village to conscript all the young men. When they see the farmer's son with his broken leg, they leave him behind. The neighbours congratulate the farmer on his good luck. His answer, of course, was simply: 'Good luck? Bad luck? Who knows?' If we allow him, then, God can use even things that seem terrible on the surface. We must try to leave it to God to decide what is good fortune and what is misfortune. By doing so, we learn the art of accepting our lives as they are, and trusting that, in the big scheme of things, God's plan will prevail.

Yet, in those more difficult times of our journeys, it is certainly hard to discern any greater plan. The fact that divine purpose and presence is so often unclear, however, does not mean that there is no plan. As a child I used to help my old Welsh *taid* ('granddad') on his remote Anglesey farm. He would tell me to do all sorts of things, from moving bales of hay to opening and closing gates at certain times of the day. In reality, I understood very little of how my actions were contributing to the workings of the farm. Still, I got on with my jobs, trusting my *taid* that I was, in some small way, contributing to the everyday running of the farm. So it is with our lives. We all interact with each other and with nature, without knowing God's greater plan. Still, we must learn to trust that, on this farm that is the world, God has a plan that will lead eventually to a wonderful harvest. Only then will our own role in this great 'theo-drama', in the words of theologian Urs von Balthasar, become clear to us.

Until that time, however, God is simply asking us to trust him. When we cannot see any reason behind events that happen, when life seems unfair, when bad things happen to good people, we must simply have faith in him. This is the only path to peace of heart. On the walls of the catacombs in Rome, the paintings reveal a remarkable serenity in the faces of early Christians. Their lack of anxiety is all the more marked when we remember how close to persecution and death they were. Jesus' life and teaching, after all, ushered in a radically new way of perceiving the world. Yet, today, as we battle against the tumult of modern life, rarely do we reach such an over-arching acceptance and peace. We must, therefore, learn to recapture that wonderful acceptance of divine purpose and that affirmation of a greater plan, even if that design is so often difficult for us to discern. We must remember, after all, that God writes straight, but with crooked lines.

Letting go

The whole process of trusting God's plan and accepting our circumstances can be summarized in one short phrase – 'letting go'. We certainly cannot conquer affliction by agonizing over it. That will merely add to our suffering. Still, most of us waste so much of our precious lives with burdens, concerns and anxieties. 'Who says worry doesn't help?' I once overheard someone quip. 'It certainly does help – every time I worry about something it doesn't happen!' Yet, if we admit that control is an illusion, and if we trust that God has a plan, letting go of our worries will allow us to participate more fully in the peace and joy of the present moment. We need, therefore, to let go and trust that the current of God's river of life knows where it is flowing. We need to let go, and let God carry us through our anxieties. We need to let go and let God.

It is, however, certainly not easy to let go in the midst of suffering and pain. Our minds, after all, race from one subject to the next and have been trained to cling to everything and anything.

This has become so deeply rooted in our psyche, and so integral to our lives, that we find it so difficult to give up our addiction to thoughts. Furthermore, letting go is so alien to us that most of us have very little concept of how liberating and life-changing it can be. So, like learning to ride a bicycle, we need to stop fighting against gravity and momentum, and, like learning to swim, we need to trust that we will float if we stop struggling and just let go. We need simply, then, to let go of our regrets of the past, to let go of our worries about the future, and to let go of the burden of comparing our lives with those of others. We need to let go and let God.

Most of all, however, we need to let go of our expectations in life, which have been drummed into us from an early age. Like the rotund rabbits in Richard Adams's *Watership Down*, we are taught from childhood that the sole purpose in life is to be comfortable and happy. Worse still, our society teaches us to believe that it is our 'right' to be healthy, successful and without pain or difficulty. Yet, expecting happiness and comfort as a God-given right is merely setting ourselves up for disappointment. If our aim in life is simply to satisfy selfish desires or to pursue a egotistical freedom from suffering, we will find ourselves chasing non-existent gold at the bottom of rainbows of false promise. We need, rather, to learn to accept that, in our life journeys, happiness will be laced with sorrow and adversity as a matter of course. There is, as the Preacher of Ecclesiastes tells us, a time and season for everything, whether pleasant or unpleasant. We need, therefore, to cease striving for the temporary fix of 'happiness'. We need rather to accept whatever circumstances we face and to cherish the grace that we do find in our daily lives. We need, ultimately, to let go and let God.

Radical acceptance

Through trusting God's plan and letting go of concerns and worries, we can even reach a degree of acceptance that makes our lot not merely tolerable, but also a joy in its own right. Such a gratitude for what we are enduring is certainly not masochistic in its origin. Rather, it is a joy that utilizes our awareness of the awe and wonder of the present moment. We do not enjoy the pain itself, but we thrive on the moments of grace that the pain brings into being. By accepting our circumstances of the present moment, then, we can start to approach the past and future in the words of Dag Hammarskjöld, one-time winner of the Nobel Peace Prize: 'For all that has been, thanks; For all that will be, yes.' Even in the torment of the Nazi concentration camp, Frankl trained himself to appreciate certain moments of each day. This was not merely a passive gratitude when suffering was lessened, termed by Schopenhauer 'negative happiness'. There were also real positive pleasures that he gleaned during his time of trial. Through nature, laughter, memory, art and other people, Frankl experienced hope in the midst of hatred and he subsequently attempted to bring meaning to the lives of other prisoners. Likewise, in Buchenwald concentration camp, the French political activist Jacques Lusseyran also affirmed hope and meaning among his fellow prisoners. Earlier in his life he had been struck blind during childhood. 'Every day since then,' he later wrote, 'I have thanked heaven for making me blind while I was still a child.' Such a rejection of pessimistic fatalism re-emerged while incarcerated at Buchenwald. His continued refusal to evade or avoid suffering inspired hope and optimism in his fellow prisoners, as he helped motivate a paradoxical spirit of both acceptance and resistance among them.

Such examples of radical acceptance suggest that our circumstances, however tragic, need not dictate our thoughts and feelings. We certainly have a choice of how we view our lives, whether through the lens of pity and regret or through the lens of hope and joy. If we let go of the desire to control, and if we accept that God is ultimately in command of our destinies, then our lives can embark on the journey to a peace that passes all understanding, as Paul puts it in his letter to the Philippians (4.7). Yet, it is certainly not easy for us to follow the path taken by the fourteenth-century mystic Julian of Norwich, who was so grateful for her hard times that she thanked God for the 'gift of her illness'. Sometimes, however, the only way for us to discover peace of mind is to reach some kind of grateful acceptance of life's ups *and* downs. The baseball star Lou Gehrig, the entertainer Roy Castle and the actors Christopher Reeve and Michael J. Fox, for example, are all famous for viewing their serious illnesses with hope and positivity, with the latter even naming his autobiography *Lucky Man*.

Our lives, after all, are rather like our children. We cannot choose our offspring, and neither can we abandon them or replace them. Rather, we love them dearly, however bad or good they turn out. Similarly, radical acceptance avoids placing any conditions on reality. Whether we face circumstances that are bad or good, we have to train ourselves to love our journeys. On the first day of a retreat I attended, the course director asked us to spend the morning reflecting on all the positive things in our lives and to thank God for those blessings. The next morning, the director surprised us all by instructing us to spend that morning reflecting on all the suffering in our lives and to thank God for all our trials and agonies too. If we can get to a position where we can do that, in spite of the terrible suffering that many of us have been through, or are going through, then that can lay foundations for a truly lasting peace of heart.

It is, then, when we start accepting the dandelions and weeds in our gardens, and even growing to love them, that we will find peace, hope and meaning in our lives. It is when we recognize that God's thoughts are not our thoughts, and his ways are not our ways, that we can start to be grateful for our lives as they are at this very moment, and we can start to accept his greater plan. *This* is radical acceptance: the belief that, whatever we are going through, God's plan will win through eventually. After all, the mystics of all the major religions agree on one thing, and that is the wonderful paradox that, no matter how dreadful life gets, in the words of Julian of Norwich, 'All shall be well and all shall be well, and all manner of things shall be well.'

Building a temple of hope and meaning

It is, therefore, through the twin-foundations of awareness of the present moment and acceptance of our present circumstances that we can start to discover hope and meaning in the chaos of suffering. Rather than pining for what we do not have, we accept where our journey has taken us and we become aware of God's grace in gifts that hitherto have been left unappreciated. Thus, we reject the illusion of a life free from suffering. Despite the numerous medical and social advances of the past century, we *all* still suffer. What we increasingly lack, however, is an awareness of transcendence in our suffering. We either put up with our afflictions or complain bitterly about them. As such, we often fail to learn from, or grow through, our difficult times.

Having laid the foundations for resurrection, then, we now move on to the building blocks of hope and meaning. Rather than numbing our thoughts and senses in an attempt to eradicate our suffering, we actually turn to experiencing the present moment more intensely. Five specific areas will be explored, although countless further life-affirming signs of transcendence could be cited. The five areas chosen – nature, laughter, memory, art and helping other people – are those implicit in Frankl's reflection on hope during the horror of the Holocaust. Each area, however, will also be shown to be firmly rooted in the biblical tradition. Through building this temple of hope and meaning, it is my hope that, however large or comparatively small your present suffering, you will be able to thank God, not for the suffering itself, but, in the words of Gerald W. Hughes, for 'its effect on you, bringing you more in touch with the enduring melody that is the intimate presence of God with you always, accompanying you in your sense of abandonment'.

4

Building blocks: nature

'The place in the monastery which is closest to God is not the church but the garden. There the monks are at their happiest'
St Pachomius, fourth-century Egyptian abbot

'You're wrong if you think the joy of life comes principally from human relationships. God's placed it all around us – it's in everything we can experience. People just need to change the way they look at those things'
Emile Hirsch as Chris McCandless in Into the Wild *(2007)*

Introduction

The Danish philosopher Søren Kierkegaard related a parable of a peasant driving a rich man in his opulent, lighted carriage. The peasant, sitting outside in the dark behind the horse, had to brave the cold and changeable weather. He also had less comfortable seating arrangements and could not rest or sleep until they reached their destination. Yet it is precisely because the rich man sat inside the carriage, in the glow of artificial light, that he missed the wonderful, breath-taking panorama of stars that the peasant was blessed to experience. Likewise, it is a paradox that it is often through our times of difficulty and suffering that our eyes can be opened to beauty that we previously missed or simply took for granted.

Even in our darkest moments, glimpses of the healing beauties of nature can bring hope and meaning to our lives. Viktor Frankl claims he experienced the wonder of nature as never before in Nazi concentration camps. Despite the terrible suffering, or maybe precisely because of it, he was 'carried away by nature's beauty'. He describes those breath-taking moments of beauty, when he and fellow prisoners would be moved by the setting sun through the Bavarian woods, by a bird landing on the barracks window, or by a light of a distant farmhouse breaking through the grey of a dawning morning. These everyday scenes took on great significance, as it drew them away from contemplation of imminent death and helped them to transcend the hopelessness of the situation. '*Et lux in tenebris lucet*', he concludes, 'and the light shineth in the darkness'.

If we allow it, then, we can experience the wonder of nature as a series of powerful moments that fill our beings with awe. Despite many of us possessing rigidly scientific mindsets, the world around us continues to inspire us to feel a deep sense of spirituality. One of the oldest Christian hymns, the *Phos Hilarion* ('O Gladsome Light'), celebrates the moment of sheer joy and amazement that one feels when the smouldering disk of the sun slowly disappears beyond the distant horizon. It is in moments such as those that the beauty of nature becomes an echo of transcendence, and does indeed lead many of us towards praise and thanksgiving.

The power of nature

I was blessed to grow up around beautiful scenery, in the small town of Penmaenmawr in North Wales. From my childhood home's front door we would enjoy spectacular views of the rolling sea. From the back door, we would stand in awe of the majestic peaks of Snowdonia. Even the poet Dylan Thomas waxed lyrical about Penmaenmawr's mountain. In *Under Milk Wood*, of all the peaks of Wales, the character Revd Eli Jenkins cites 'Penmaenmawr defiant' as towering like a giant in comparison to lowly Llareggub Hill. Thus, my childhood was blessed with frequent opportunities to marvel at the wonder of nature. Our own proximity to countryside, however, need not dictate our sense of appreciation for nature. In fact, living in a rural area can often lead us to take our natural surroundings for granted.

In reality, whether we reside in the country or in an urban area, we all are presented with ample opportunities to experience moments of intense awareness of the beauty of creation. One can certainly be left in awe by a breath-taking scenic view, but one can also be similarly moved by a simple hedge in a park, a leaf on a household plant or a bird in the sky. After all, appreciating the wonder of nature is not related to geographical proximity, but is rather a way of seeing and perceiving. As William Blake noted: 'The tree which moves some to tears of joy is, in the eyes of others, only a green thing which stands in the way. As a man is, so he sees.'

Our education system in the United Kingdom recognizes that, at a young age, children are naturally inclined towards a sense of awe and wonder at the world and at nature. Spiritual, moral, social and cultural development of pupils is incorporated into the subjects of the curriculum in order to affirm and develop such awareness. As we grow older, the freshness of this wonderment is often drained away from us. Yet, even the most humanist of scientists acknowledge that in the face of the mystery, beauty and complexity of the Universe words like 'awe' and 'wonder' come quite naturally to us. As a result, environmentalists, even those who have long abandoned faith, continue to use biblical phrases such as 'sacred' and 'stewardship' to affirm their dedication to nature, while scientists are increasingly reintroducing elements of mystery and wonder into their ways of speaking of nature. 'We all of us', noted celebrated atheist Richard Dawkins, in a public debate with Christian mathematician John Lennox, 'share a kind of religious reverence for the beauties of the Universe.' This, of course, does not mean scientists are turning to Christianity in their droves, but certainly some could be regarded as becoming more spiritual in the broadest sense of the term. In contemplating the awesomeness of the universe, as the film *3:10 to Yuma* (2007) puts it, 'sometimes a man's got to be big enough to see how small he is'.

By recovering the sense of awe at creation, so freely present during our childhood, we take a step towards experiencing the natural world as a source of hope and meaning in our turbulent lives. Our rediscovery of beauty and mystery in the natural world can, after all, help provide fresh perspectives on our troubles. When Oscar Wilde was released from prison, he immediately visited the seaside. He reflected on this with a quote by Euripides: 'The sea washes away the stains and wounds of the world.' A positive awareness of nature, then, can lift our spirits, can still and calm our afflicted and restless minds, and can help us learn to let go of worries and anxieties.

The Bible and nature

After each day in the Genesis account of creation, God sees that what he has formed is *tov*, a Hebrew word meaning good, pleasurable and delightful. At the end of the creative process, he then looks at the whole of his handiwork, and he sees that the wonderful harmony of the complex, intricate and balanced ecosystem is *tov me'od*, meaning 'very good'. Christ later tells us that only God himself is good, so it follows that creation can, in some way, reveal the goodness of God directly to us. It is no surprise, then, that the natural world figures prominently in the Bible.

The Hebrew authors of the Ancient Near East themselves experienced a rich biodiversity, and their appreciation of nature is clear from their writings. In fact, it has been argued that the Old Testament is firstly a book about nature, and only secondly a book about man. The Mosaic laws, for example, give such detailed rules on caring for trees and forests that some commentators have seen in Deuteronomy 20.19 the world's first nature protection regulation and in Numbers 35.2ff. the first legal formation of greenbelts around cities. The Israelites are likewise warned that they should not defile or pollute their environment (Num. 35.33ff.). After all, God himself is regarded as inhabiting the land. Elsewhere in the Old Testament, odes to the natural world are frequent and joyous (cf. Psalms, Song of Songs), while the detail and intricacy of Job's celebration of nature shows the author of the book to be a skilled naturalist.

In the New Testament, God's involvement with nature is taken a step further, with the whole concept of the incarnation. God clothes himself in human flesh, as he personally treads the earth and interacts with the natural world. Jesus' special relationship with the created order is revealed in the fact that his parables, miracles and sayings are infused with nature and pastoral imagery. He was, after all, a man who was rooted in the first-century landscape of vineyards, rocks, weeds, birds, wheat crops, sheep, seeds, wild flowers, rivers, seas and fish. In the Sermon on the Mount he confirms that nature is under God's providence, and even urges his listeners to emulate other living things – the lilies of the field and the birds of the sky. Christ even chose to spend his last moments of freedom in a garden, and then made his first resurrection appearance in another garden, where he was mistaken for a gardener.

The presence of Jesus in the natural order of things was certainly something that the early Church recognized, as it regarded him as the 'true vine', the 'good shepherd' and the 'living water'. Furthermore, the monastic fathers followed Christ's lead in viewing the wilderness as their place of prayer and contemplation. The desert was traditionally regarded as a place of spiritual warfare, where mystics battled their demons. It was also for them, though, the local countryside, where they could be still and connect to God, just as the hermits of Russia headed for the vast forests of their own landscape. Members of religious orders, however, did not need to retreat to the extremities of the desert or forest to discover the fingerprints of a living God in creation. St Benedict, the founder of Western monasticism, encouraged his followers to spend time both working and praying in the garden, and gardening became a mainstay of monastic communities down the ages. Rarely do contemporary Christians, when they feel drawn towards the wild beauty, awe and wonder of nature, realize how closely this mirrors both the biblical and monastic experience.

Theology and nature

Despite the positive biblical and monastic view of the created order, theologians and church leaders have traditionally been rather blasé or even antagonistic towards nature. The theological development of a radical transcendent deity, distinct and separate from his creation, resulted from the belief that creation is fallen and corrupt, combined with a deep-seated fear of pagan animism and pantheism. From the time of Augustine, theology largely tended towards a dualism of matter and spirit, and the Protestant Reformers would later champion God as the Lord of History, rather than the Lord of Creation. While the downplaying of nature was at odds with biblical evidence, it soon became orthodox teaching within churches in the West.

Certainly, we need to ensure that we do not descend into pantheistic belief. God is infinitely more than his creation, and so he cannot be simply identified with it. The eighth-century Chinese poet Li Bai is said to have loved the moon so much that he drowned trying to embrace its reflection in the river. Similarly, if we start worshipping nature itself, we are only witnessing one aspect of the divine and so are setting ourselves up for a fall. Yet, God's incarnation is not limited to the Word made flesh in Jesus. The divine is certainly present in all physical things, and so we must be open to hear his voice in bird song, to taste his presence in our fauna and forests, and to see his touch in the remarkable delicacy of a blossoming flower. 'Everything that lives is holy,' wrote William Blake; 'life delights in life.'

Such a realization can lead us to recover a new and refreshed natural theology, where our concept of God includes the world, but also exceeds it. Christ has an independent identity from his creation, but he is also 'all, and in all' (Col. 3.11). Nature can, therefore, help lead us to the divine. After all, God is, in the words of Thomas Aquinas, *summum bonum*, the sum of all goodness, which includes his creation. 'There are two books from whence I collect my divinity,' wrote the physician Sir Thomas Browne in his 1643 classic *Religio Medici*, 'beside that written one of God, another of his servant, nature, that universal and publick manuscript, that lies expansed unto the eyes of all.'

The Eastern Orthodox Churches have long held such a sacramental view of nature, believing that all matter is charged with God's power. As a result, a distinction is drawn between God's transcendent essence, which lies beyond our experience, and his divine energy, which permeates all that exists. We need, therefore, to recover the immanence and transcendence of a God who is both *in* and *beyond* nature. After all, it is when we recognize the existence of something beyond this world that we are truly able to appreciate the created order in its fullness. To treat the world around us as the sum of everything will paradoxically lead us to lose something of its wonder. As C. S. Lewis puts it: 'The Englishness of English is audible only to those who know some other language as well.'

God's relationship with nature is, then, incarnational, sacramental and dynamic. Matter is part of the divine milieu and God's energy dwells within the created order. A popular image to express this relationship, both in Scripture (cf. Ps. 114 and Isa. 55.12) and in the medieval Christian tradition, is the dance of creation. Physical, inanimate objects, such as trees and mountains, are pictured dancing with joy in the presence of the divine. The recent discovery from quantum physics, that at a sub-atomic level all particles are in a state of constant flux and movement, fits neatly with this image. The ground of our universe is now considered to be completely dynamic, with particles continually disappearing and then re-emerging. As long as creation exists, the dance goes on.

Contemporary science can, likewise, be seen as lending credence to the theological concept of continuous creation. The universe, we are now told, is less determined and mechanistic than was previously believed. The theory of evolution implies continuous change, while quantum physics holds that at a sub-atomic level even inanimate matter has some kind of free will, which offers it a range of possibilities at all times. Continuous creativity is therefore interwoven through the basic fabric of God's creation. Christian theology, of course, asserts that God is not only the creator, but also the sustainer of all that exists. God's work was not limited to the flourish of activity in the first six days of creation. Rather, he continually nurtures and nourishes his handiwork, in an ongoing process of fresh creativity. 'My father is working still,' Christ asserted, 'and I am working' (John 5.17).

With this fresh concept of natural theology, everything has the potential to be *theophanic*. Everything can reveal the divine presence to us. As the nineteenth-century poet Elizabeth Barrett Browning wrote in her poem 'Aurora Leigh':

> Earth's crammed with heaven,
> And every common bush afire with God;
> But only he who sees takes off his shoes,
> The rest sit round it and pluck blackberries.

If only we open our eyes and ears, every tree, every flower, every bird, every mountain, every blade of grass can burst into flames and offer us an encounter with the transcendent.

Awareness of the natural world

The Celtic Church believed that God's creation was littered with 'thin places', where the veil between the natural and supernatural was slight. To appreciate the wonder of the divine in these places, however, it was held that individuals needed to attune their minds to God's presence. Awareness of the transcendent quality in nature was, for Celtic monastics, very much part of their personal devotion and worship. 'Pleasant to me is the glittering of the sun today upon these margins,' wrote one tenth-century Gaelic monk on the side of his manuscript. Yet, in today's world, our busy, world-weary and often cynical mindsets often fail to recognize, or take time to notice, the wonder of our natural surroundings. We are, as Gerard Manley Hopkins reminded us, increasingly blind to the grandeur of God in creation.

We need, therefore, to recover our appreciation of the presence of God in midst of his handiwork. Nature is a sacred, living temple and, just as art reveals something of the artist, creation reveals something of the Creator. In his *Confessions*, Augustine claims that there was a time when things of beauty seduced him away from their maker. Later, however, these same things drew him ever closer to their source. 'Too late have I loved you,' he wrote, 'O beauty so ancient and so new.' An awareness and appreciation of nature can, then, certainly unite us with the creative force behind everything, and can inspire us to know and love the creator more fully.

Such an awareness of nature can also have the effect of reminding us how fragile, dependent and mortal we are. In one of her revelations, Julian of Norwich was shown how the whole of creation was like something as small as a hazelnut. The delicateness and fragility of that diminutive nut, as it lay in the palm of her hand, revealed to her how God's love sustains and preserves all that exists. Such a realization of our dependence on God is at the root of acceptance. Nature can certainly teach us about accepting the reality we face and letting go of our worries and concerns. While animals display signs that they are in pain and even in distress, in his poem 'Self Pity', D. H. Lawrence highlights the fact that they never feel sorry for themselves. A bird, for example, will live its life and finally 'drop frozen dead from a bough' having not experienced remorse, worry or self-pity. Christ himself recognized this to be the case, as he encouraged us to learn the art of acceptance and trust from the natural world. After all, the lilies of the field and the birds in the sky do not have sleepless nights of worry, and do not need therapy or pharmaceutical drugs to allay their anxious minds. Paradoxically, acceptance is also fostered as we observe the inevitability of decay and death in nature. The seasons come and the seasons go, while the natural world calmly accepts its fate – from blooming growth to rotting decay, before the cycle begins again. Thus, through embracing God's providence, we accept the certainty of decline and deterioration, but look forward with hope to spring after winter and new life after death.

We are also helped to let go of our concerns when we recognize that we are, ultimately, part and parcel of nature, rather than self-contained isolated egos. The world is, essentially, a living organism of interconnected, mutually dependent elements. The current groans of our global environment, which we have cruelly and blindly mistreated for so long, starkly demonstrate our shared fate with the natural world. All that thrives in our enormous ecosystem is connected. Nothing is foreign or alien to us. We all belong – to each other, to the animals, and to the trees and plants. Not one of us is alone and adrift in this universe. In the past, theology has all too often championed the individual over the corporate. As the body of Christ, however, we are all united and intricately bound with all creation.

God, then, stands at the centre of our reciprocal universe, as its life-blood. He creates and sustains all things – the merciless and dreadful alongside the wonderful and life-affirming. 'Did He who made the Lamb make thee?' William Blake asked the raging tiger. Such a realization of our oneness with each other and with nature can help us engender a sense of distance and perspective on our suffering. It, therefore, makes the acceptance of our present lot so much more bearable. Frankl describes how one young prisoner, who knew she had only days left to live, used her sense of harmony with nature to come to an acceptance of her bleak circumstances. Pointing to a chestnut tree, she told Frankl that she often talked to that tree. He asked her if the tree, with its scattered blossoms, ever replied. 'Yes,' she answered. 'It said to me, "I am here – I am here – I am life, eternal life."'

Through awareness and acceptance, nature can certainly help nourish and heal us. In the winter of 1939 the famous explorer W. H. Murray visited the remote Lost Valley, near Glencoe in the Highlands of Scotland. He wrote that in the midst of such beauty 'the natural movement' of the heart was to 'lift upward'. In our recognition of the divine mystery in the wonder of creation, then, our hearts are uplifted and we transcend our mundane concerns, shortcomings and petty conflicts. At times of great sadness especially, nature draws us closer to the divine and offers us glimpses of hope and healing. After all, when we place ourselves in the presence of beauty and become aware of the infusion of transcendence in that beauty, we cannot fail to be transformed. We are, after all, part of the same world that changes a caterpillar into a butterfly and the vicious forest fire into an opportunity for new life. Transformation is at the very heart of nature.

Encountering God in nature

We can, then, discover transcendence through the beauty and goodness of creation. Nature is like a radio station, continually broadcasting God to us. All we need to do is to tune in to its frequency. Instead of losing our sense of wonder as we grow older, our eyes can be opened further to the mystery and awe of what is familiar to us and what is new. Even our awareness of the very ordinariness of nature can change our whole perception of scenes and moments we have grown to take for granted. As C. S. Lewis reflected in a letter to his childhood friend Arthur Greeves, following a walk in the countryside:

> The same winter sunshine, the same gilt and grey skies shining through bare shock-headed bushes, the same restful pale ploughland and

grass, and more than usual of the birds darting out their sudden, almost cruelly poignant songs – today I got such a sudden intense feeling of delight that it sort of stopped me in my walk and spun me round.

We must certainly be wary not to sentimentalize nature or to read into it a projection of our own hopes and ideals. 'Plenty of people say they love nature on Sundays, when the weather is fine and they are then carried away by their own sentiment,' wrote Hermann Hesse in *Peter Camenzind*. Yet, neither should we allow the suffering and sacrifice of nature, which makes it red in tooth and claw, blind us from its accompanying beauty and wonder. Both Jesus in the wilderness and the monastic fathers in the deserts of Egypt would certainly have witnessed the cruelty and bleakness of the natural world, but they still recognized that its majesty and wonder reflected the creator.

In *In the Name of the Father* (1993), the film adaptation of the wrongful imprisonment of the Guildford Four, Gerry Conlon, played by Daniel Day-Lewis, maintains that, in the monotony and pain of prison, 'a snowstorm is like a present from God'. Despite any darkness we may be going through, we can certainly still find light through the gift of his creation. In fact, it is often when we are pushed off course from our normal habits or timetables, whether through suffering or another reason, that we discover a new ability to truly notice the natural world around us, rather than blindly passing by on our way to do something else. My father, who served as a parish priest in North Wales, relates a tale about a parishioner he used to visit in a nursing home. This elderly man told my dad that he had never appreciated the wonder of nature during his busy working life in the famous granite quarry of Penmaenmawr. His life, however, had been changed beyond description when, after retirement, his wife had died and his house and all his belongings were destroyed in the great floods that hit the North Wales coast in the early 1990s. Eventually, he ended up bedbound in a residential home. It was then, he claimed, that he began to appreciate his natural surroundings, as the view from his window – of the sweeping, majestic mountains of Snowdonia – became his lifeline and his one joy as he faced his decline. Each and every morning, when his curtains were opened, he would recite aloud Psalm 121.1 – 'I lift up mine eyes unto the hills, from whence cometh my help.' At his funeral service, my father was surprised to see the entire nursing home staff present. 'Each day I'd open those bedroom curtains for him,' one care worker told my father, 'and I'll never again take the beauty of my surroundings for granted.'

We need, then, to take time to feel, experience and appreciate the divine energy exuding from the natural world. This is the holy energy of the first day of creation, and when we behold a leaf, a stone or a scene of nature, it is as if it is being recreated all over again. As such, we bring it to a new birth and, for that moment, it becomes our whole world. We can therefore look at it and see that it is *tov*, as we experience first hand its inherent goodness and open ourselves to the source of this beauty and the sustainer of this delight.

We, therefore, learn the importance of delighting in creation and soaking up its beauty like a sponge. One Jewish thinker suggested that the first and only question God will ask us at the final judgement will be: 'Did you enjoy my creation?' For us to be able to answer in the affirmative, we must root ourselves in the present moment and live with our eyes open to beauty in all its manifest forms. When we only take time to notice, the divine can be immediately and powerfully present to us in the natural world. Little wonder, then, that Welsh poet R. S. Thomas, in the poem 'The Bright Field', compares those breath-taking moments of awareness to the 'pearl of great price' of the Gospel parable (Matt. 13.45–6):

> I have seen the sun break through
> to illuminate a small field
> for a while, and gone my way
> and forgotten it. But that was the pearl
> of great price . . .
> Life is not hurrying
> on to a receding future, nor hankering after
> an imagined past. It is the turning
> aside like Moses to the miracle
> of the lit bush.

5

Building blocks: laughter

'Life does not cease to be funny when someone dies any more than
it ceases to be serious when someone laughs'

George Bernard Shaw

'If you can find humour in anything, you can survive it'

Bill Cosby

Introduction

On 24 July 2008, the comedian Roy Walker, one-time presenter
of the popular TV gameshow *Catchphrase*, was being interviewed
on BBC Breakfast News about his recent comeback. Encouraged
by the presenter Siân Williams to 'tell us a joke', Walker told a tale
about his grandfather who had fought on the beaches of Normandy
during the Second World War. 'The index finger on his right hand
was missing,' Walker jested, 'so he couldn't pull a trigger and he
was the worst shot on the firing range. So he said to the sergeant
major, "Does this mean I won't be going over to France?" and the
sergeant major replied, "No, it actually means you won't be coming back!"' At the punchline, there followed a painful silence in
the BBC studio. Later, Siân Williams apologized to Walker with a
revealing explanation: 'It's because it was about death; I thought
"I'd better not laugh – I can't laugh at something like that."'

Society certainly teaches us that there are moments in life that
are sacrosanct. We are taught that these moments are, in some
sense, beyond humour. The association of the word 'laughter' with
words such as 'suffering', 'death' or 'pain' seems oxymoronic and
offensive. Yet, on the evidence of it, suffering and laughter are not
so polarized in our lives. Even in the horrors of the Holocaust,

Viktor Frankl writes of the 'grim sense of humour' that helped him and others survive. Naturally, humour was not widespread in the camps, but on occasion it did break through in an unexpected and astonishing way, if only 'for a few seconds or minutes'. On an unforgiving hard labour site, where the foreman would continually shout 'action! action!' to encourage a faster work rate, Frankl recalls laughing with a former surgeon at the thought of being back in the operating room after the war, with someone shouting 'action! action!' as he performed a difficult abdominal operation.

Laughter, then, certainly does not happen in times of pleasure and joy alone. Even in moments of intense suffering, laughter can break through to soothe our wounds. A definitive separation between humour and suffering is not only unrealistic, but is also detrimental to healing. A failure to recognize humour in our daily struggles can leave us lacking hope and meaning in otherwise hopeless situations. We need, then, to take time to step back and notice the comedic aspects of our lives. We need to learn to laugh despite our everyday struggles and miseries. After all, as G. K. Chesterton wrote, 'the reason angels can fly is because they take themselves lightly'.

Finding laughter in suffering

From the earliest civilizations until very recently, it has been assumed that laughter is a fundamental feature that distinguishes humans from other creatures. Thus, it was noted that animals such as the kookaburra and the hyena merely have a phonetic similarity to human laughter and so humankind was regarded as, in the words of Aristotle, 'the creature who laughs'. Recent research, however, suggests that apes may 'smile' and 'laugh' when responding to pleasure stimuli. Still, the universality, subtlety and complexity of humankind's 'humour' differentiates it from any possible basic 'laughter' of primitive animals. As such, our sense of humour is a luxury afforded to us as a biologically secure species. Laughter does not, after all, act to preserve or propagate life. It could, therefore, be said that not to laugh is to cease to be human.

The other luxury reflex that humans possess is crying, and increasingly scientists are recognizing a very close connection between laughter and crying. Both are directly affected by the perception of the mind and both have physiological components located in the adrenal system. It should, therefore, come as no surprise that suffering and laughter have a close relationship. Anyone who has watched a Woody Allen film will recognize that life's daily anxieties can stand quite naturally, in art at least, alongside a comic celebration of that life. One need only look at the actual lives of many famous comedians to see that this attitude is not reserved to the imaginative arts. So many of the world's greatest comics have had unhappy childhoods, through isolation, depression or loss. Yet they gained power over their suffering through humour. Suffering can certainly make us more serious, but that seriousness often deepens our humour. Actor Mike Myers, star of *Austin Powers* and voice of *Shrek*, for example, posits his darkest moments as the source of his humour. 'Nothing's so bad it can't be laughed at,' he recalls his dad telling him. Years later his dad would live out his philosophy, as he battled Alzheimer's with bravery and humour. 'So strong and innately human is the need to laugh,' concludes Myers.

In fact, humour, more than anything else in the human make-up, gives us an ability to rise above situations and keep us going despite our unhappiness or suffering. After all, without a recognition of the humorous side of life, we start to view situations literally and one-dimensionally, thus becoming mere victims. Evidence of laughter in the most extreme circumstances is widespread. Ministry of Defence psychologists, for example, recount the importance of humour at all levels of the UK armed forces in recent conflicts. The conflict in Iraq also saw a widely reported example of the interplay of laughter and suffering, when in 2005 four Western Christian peacemakers were kidnapped. The magazine *Sojourners* reported that, alongside the tears of worry and frustration, the colleagues of the kidnapped four found time to laugh. The running joke at the Christian Peacemaker Team headquarters was that the kidnappers must be men, because 'we gave them our phone number, but they haven't called us'. Some of the men on the team, however, retorted with their own running joke that the kidnappers must be 'women that the Christian Peacemaker Team had wronged – that's why they're giving us the silent treatment'.

Rather than being inappropriate, as it might at first seem, such laughter could be regarded as a necessary human response to the painful enormity of the situation. Even at a local, everyday level, those involved in pastoral work often experience times when laughter is helpful or healing. For example, while the old Celtic wakes, with their open coffins and joyous mourning, are largely a thing of the past, the tears and the visible pain of grief are still often accompanied by smiles, laughter and memories, with funeral eulogies offering an opportunity for amusing anecdotes alongside more sombre words. Likewise, hospices for the dying and homes for the elderly are places where we can experience both the most harrowing moments of ministry and some of the most unexpected and refreshing laughter. 'The greatest commandment is love God,' I read confidently during a service at one hospice, 'and the second is this: Love your neighbour.' Without warning, a woman at the back of the room shouted, 'I don't love my neighbour.' As I was briefly rendered speechless, the moment of silence gave the woman the opportunity to add something else: 'And, listen 'ere, vicar, if *you* knew her, *you* wouldn't love her either.' A place that was so often steeped in darkness, frustration and grief was, for a brief moment, united in one of God's most healing gifts – laughter.

Theories of laughter

One of the earliest theories of laughter, the 'superiority theory', has little relevance to any theology of suffering and humour. A number of the ancient Greek and Roman philosophers, such as Plato, Aristotle and Cicero, maintained that our laughter makes us feel better, but does so almost exclusively at the expense of those who are weak, powerless or ignorant. Humour can certainly be rooted in cruelty and dominance, but this cannot help us find hope or meaning in our suffering. Other theories of laughter, however, seek to affirm humour as a necessary and healthy response to suffering. The 'incongruity theory', developed by thinkers such as Kant, Schopenhauer and Kierkegaard, maintains that we laugh at what is absurd. There is, then, an inter-relationship between paradox and laughter. This is the topsy-turvydom of humour, emphasized by the French philosopher Henri Bergson. Tragic situations are certainly not funny in themselves, but laughter is drawn out of the absurdity of the circumstances. For Christians this directly relates to theodicy. Suffering, in light of a loving God, is indeed absurd. To laugh about our predicaments, however, demonstrates that the self is not totally engulfed by the seeming pointlessness of our struggles. Laughter, then, opposes the one-dimensional thinking that equates suffering with hopelessness.

Sigmund Freud, on the other hand, saw laughter as a way of dissipating and relieving emotional tension. From his work has developed the 'psychological relief theory'. Thus, humour becomes an important coping tool for individuals, as it gives a new perspective that helps deal with difficulties. Jacqueline Bussie builds upon this to see laughter as 'a mode of resistance'. As such, laughter has allowed those enduring great pain and tragedy to transcend their predicaments, as they are lifted above fear, hopelessness and despair. In a seminal study, Bussie analyses the books of Elie Wiesel, Toni Morrison and Shusaku Endo to demonstrate that even in the horrors of genocide, slavery and religious persecution, laughter becomes a source of strength, protest and therapeutic defiance.

Humour is, then, a valuable resource for inner healing. Laughter provides powerful cathartic cleansing and is an important mechanism for releasing stress and tension. Numerous contemporary authors have, therefore, posited humour as essential to transcending our suffering and to overcoming life's emotional crises. Author Phil Simmons's journal of his struggle with the terminal motor neurone disease is revealing. For Simmons, who was diagnosed with the disease at the young age of 35, humour brought sanity, hope and light to a dark and difficult emotional journey. Sadness and comedy stand side by side in the pages of his journal. 'If we can't laugh,' the father of two young children concluded, 'we can't properly be serious.' Humour certainly takes us away from our troubles, even if only for a moment, thus making them easier to bear. Alongside this, the physiological benefits of laughter are widely attested. Laughter, after all, triggers the release of oxytocin in the brain and causes a rush of endorphins, the body's natural painkiller. Thus, it makes us feel more relaxed and can, according to one study, boost our body's immune system. A further study claims that the increase in heart rate during hearty laughter is as beneficial to health as 15 minutes of exercise. Little wonder, then, that laughter-therapist Allen Klein suggests that we should ensure we are taking a daily dose of Vitamin 'H' ('humour') alongside our more traditional vitamins and minerals.

As individuals, then, a sense of humour is imperative for emotional well-being. Yet laughter is also important for families, communities and society. After all, it is most often experienced in the company of others, and is certainly enhanced when shared. It serves to unite people in an amazing way, by generating warmth, affinity and solidarity. Through shared humour we realize that we do not stand alone in our difficult situations. With the untimely death of Diana, Princess of Wales, a true story, oft-repeated in Wales at the time, not only (to lift a phrase employed by comedian Jimmy Carr) 'punctured the suffocating atmosphere of compulsory national mourning', but also reflected the importance of laughter alongside genuine sadness. News reports of the possible role of paparazzi on mopeds in the tragic accident were widespread when a Swansea clergyman visited an elderly parishioner. On arriving at her house he found her in the process of throwing out all her opera CDs. He naturally enquired why she was discarding such an impressive collection. She answered with tears in her eyes: 'I just can't listen to him any more, vicar. The news is saying he caused the crash – that damn Pavarotti on his moped chasing poor Diana!' In a similar vein, brave comedians, such as Joan Rivers, Ricky Gervais and Stewart Lee, have dealt with issues such as Diana's death, 9/11 and the Holocaust, both to ask probing and necessary questions, and to help society face and cope with such tragedies.

Christianity and laughter

In Umberto Eco's novel *The Name of the Rose*, a Benedictine librarian finds Aristotle's lost work on comedy. Realizing the potential of humour to undermine the status quo, he poisons the pages of the manuscript. The Churches, it is thus implied, are fearful of humour because laughter is impossible to control. Christianity certainly developed as a religion where humour had a subordinate place. After all, for the most part, the Bible itself is a very serious book. Laughter in the Old Testament is ambiguous, and so it is not hard to formulate a negative theology of laughter. God does laugh, but divine laughter can be interpreted as a laughter of hatred and contempt (cf. Ps. 2.4). Isaac's name might well mean 'laughter', but this can be interpreted as the sceptical and faithless laughter of Sarah when God announced she would conceive (Gen. 18.12). Likewise, in the New Testament, not one verse attests to Christ having laughed, a fact that Nietzsche would later give as one justification for his atheism. To make matters all the worse, St Paul risked killing Christian mirth stone dead with his admonition of *eutrapelia*, sometimes translated as 'jesting', in his letter to the Ephesians (5.4).

Alongside scripture's ambiguous teaching on laughter, early theologians were influenced by the predominant Platonic Greek thought that equated laughter with ridicule. For Augustine, laughter belonged to the lower part of humankind. 'Human beings laugh and weep,' he wrote, 'and it is a matter for weeping that they laugh.' Other early Church fathers, such as Jerome, John Chrysostom and Hugh of St Victor, were as virulent in their condemnation of humour. Despite taking seriously its dialogue with science, literature and philosophy, then, theology's attitude to humour largely developed in an ambivalent or antipathetic way. Theology became a sombre matter, as laughter was regarded as either nihilistic or irresponsible. Alternatively, as Dante's *Divine Comedy* indicates, laughter became a luxury reserved for the elect in Paradise.

There is, however, another side to this seemingly depressing scenario. On visiting India a few years back, I was invited to a meal with a poverty-stricken Hindu family. To my surprise, alongside their shrine to local deities, was a large picture of Jesus, heartily laughing. This striking image of the 'laughing Jesus', in the midst of the poverty and suffering, summarized the paradox of faith. Christianity is a religion of both joy *and* sorrow. St Paul was, after all, 'sorrowful, yet always rejoicing' (2 Cor. 6.10). Joy and laughter are admittedly not identical, but they are certainly closely inter-related. Laughter can point to a happiness that transcends circumstances. That happiness and fulfilment can be defined as 'joy' and is where God's presence is found in its fullness. In the Welsh language the word '*hwyl*' has traditionally been used in the chapels to refer to religious fervour, zeal and joy. That same word is now in everyday usage to simply mean 'fun' or, when used as a departing remark, 'have fun'. Joy and laughter in Christianity are certainly blood brothers, and we can experience *hwyl*, in both senses of the word, despite the most trying of circumstances.

Once we recognize this paradoxical nature of the Christian journey, we can begin to recognize the satire, irony, riddles and amusing stories found in scripture. There are, for example, numerous Old Testament passages that present laughter in a positive light (cf. Proverbs, Ecclesiastes), and the teaching of Jesus contrasts so sharply with the conventional wisdom of first-century Israel that his words can be seen as flowing thick with irony. Theologian Harvey Cox suggests that Christ is the ultimate archetype of the 'holy fool', from his birth among animals in the stable, through his joke-like parables (complete with set-ups and punchlines), to his final days, as he rode into Jerusalem as a king on a donkey. It is, therefore, not hard for us to picture a fully human Christ smiling and laughing. After all, he continually derided the Pharisees for taking themselves too seriously. 'I'm sure Jesus himself knew how to make people laugh,' stated Michael Palin, in a recent defence of the Monty Python film *The Life of Brian* (1979), '. . . it's an odd idea that has crept in during the intervening two thousand years – that there should be no laughs in religion.' Furthermore, even St Paul's attitude to humour is being re-evaluated, with some theologians claiming that in his condemnation of *eutrapelia* in Ephesians he was not opposing urbane jesting but rather criticizing lewd talk. 'The Gospel', concluded Kierkegaard, 'represents the most humorous point of view in the history of the world.'

From the Church's earliest days there were certainly theologians, such as Pope Sixtus, St Basil, Maximus the Confessor and Thomas Aquinas, who bucked the prevalent theological trend and recognized laughter as a wonderful gift from God. At the Reformation, humour became all the more important to Christian thinkers. Luther employed laughter as a weapon to deride the papacy, while a long list of Reformation figures, including Erasmus, Thomas More, Rabelais and Melanchthon, translated classical comedies, such as those of Lucian of Samosata. Furthermore, in ecclesiastical practice, laughter played an essential role for many centuries. In the late middle ages, we witness a religion where laughter was heard quite naturally alongside roars of rage in church. Certainly by the time of the Reformation, Christian celebrations involved much merry-making and laughter. Clergy, acolytes and laity were involved in the various annual celebrations – at the Feast of Fools on or around New Year's Day, at the Medieval mystery plays, and at Shrovetide, the English equivalent of the pre-Lent carnival tradition of mainland Europe. In Germany, 'Easter Laughter' (*Risus Paschalis*) was particularly popular, as congregations were rewarded with joke-filled sermons after a season of many sad and serious lenten sermons. Predictably, however, the majority of mainstream theologians condemned such joyous celebrations.

Christianity, laughter and suffering

It seems that one of the principal reasons for the antipathy towards laughter in theological circles down the ages was the belief that a suffering world must be taken seriously. 'As long as we are in the vale of tears,' wrote Jerome in the fourth century, 'we may not laugh, but must weep.' In more recent times, Reinhold Neibuhr insisted that faith, not laughter, was the only possible response to suffering. Ironically, however, another strand of Christian thought has regarded suffering and laughter as inextricably linked. Even in the Bible itself, the book of Proverbs legitimizes the laughter of the suffering believer (Prov. 14.13) and asserts that humour is beneficial to physical well-being (Prov. 17.22). In the thirteenth century, Thomas Aquinas took this a step further by claiming that humour could also stimulate mental health. He recounted a story from John Cassian's 'Conferences of the Fathers', when John the Evangelist caused scandal through joking with his disciples. He responded to his accusers by picking up an archer's bow and asking them whether it was good to keep it continually bent. 'No,' they answered, 'it would break.' John applied that very lesson to the mind – we all need laughter and humour to unbend and relax our thoughts and emotions. Other theologians, many of whom were no strangers to suffering themselves, continued this vein of thought. At the time of the Reformation, both Erasmus and Rabelais regarded laughter as holding therapeutic powers. C. S. Lewis maintained that having 'great fun' was one of the prerequisites of the Christian journey.

To give precedence to humour does not mean, then, that we are ignoring the reality of suffering and evil in the world. Rather, according to Karl Barth, true humour 'presupposes rather than excludes the knowledge of suffering'. It is, quite literally, 'laughter amid tears'. Perhaps this would have developed as mainstream thinking had it not been for the fact that theology was written almost exclusively by white males in positions of power. From the viewpoint of the weak, oppressed and powerless a sense of humour is imperative. For these people, laughter leads to hope and protest and is therefore empowering. As such, laughter can be closely related to those scriptural passages that announce freedom for the oppressed and suffering, such as the Magnificat (Luke 1.46–55) and Christ's announcement of the year of Lord's favour (Luke 4.18–19). Laughter makes our present life endurable and it offers fresh possibilities of a new life. Like the work of the Holy Spirit, when laughter breaks through our suffering, it can transform and transfigure our situations, sometimes temporarily and sometimes permanently. 'In playing we can anticipate our liberation,' writes Jürgen Moltmann, 'and with laughing rid ourselves of the bonds which alienate us from real life.'

Awareness and acceptance

Art and nature have long been regarded in Christian theology as part of God's natural revelation. Humour, then, should also be recognized as a signal of transcendence. Laughter can break through the struggles of our lot and give us a sacramental taste of another reality. It offers us a glimpse of redemption, and it does so in a way that exalts mind, spirit and body. After all, humour originates in the mind, is manifested in the body, and lifts the spirit. It can paradoxically, therefore, be both a deeply spiritual and a firmly embodying experience.

This is the foundation of the contemplative emphasis on 'the importance of not being earnest', to borrow a phrase from Arthur Koestler. Contemplatives and mystics have, after all, long been linked to joy and laughter. While St Benedict, founder of the Benedictine movement, regarded laughter as a sign of unrighteousness and ungodliness, other prominent monastics and mystics drew inspiration from St Paul's exhortation that we should become fools for Christ's sake (cf. 1 Cor. 3.18; Phil. 4.4). St Francis of Assisi's sense of humour, for example, became legendary and Franciscans became renowned for their humour and amusing preaching, echoed most famously in the jolly Friar Tuck character of the Robin Hood legend. Other contemplatives who were notable for their praise of laughter include Julian of Norwich, who referred to rejoicing, delight and being merry in God's presence, and Meister Eckhart, who located laughter in the Trinity by suggesting that the Son and Father laugh with each other, and that laughter subsequently 'begets' the Holy Spirit.

In more recent times, the Trappist monk Thomas Merton is said to have cultivated a humorous, yet compassionate, detachment about himself and the things he regarded as important. It is such detachment that lies at the root of both awareness and healthy laughter. Both require us to step back from our personal situations, and both can therefore lead to a sense of distance, proportion and perspective. The American comedian Lenny Bruce suggested that the equation for comedy was 'laughter = pain + time'. The 'time' element of the equation, however, can also be expressed as 'distance', 'detachment' or even 'awareness'. If we allow humour to be part of our pain, then, it can expand our vision and can give us a more objective way of seeing circumstances. Far from minimizing or seeking to escape harsh reality, humour, in fact, saves us from being caught in realism, when we take everything factually and on its own terms. We, therefore, are able to cope with our problems and difficulties more adequately and even more pleasantly. This can help us to change and grow, as past ways of responding and behaving are surrendered.

In some small way, then, our sense of humour affords us a 'God's-eye view' of the tragedies of life. As such, even if there is no prospect of a 'quick fix' from our suffering, humour allows us to regain some sense of God's purpose and providential care. As a result, it helps us reach that acceptance of what is incongruous in our lives. St Francis, for example, is said to have reached such a total acceptance of God's will in his life that he would break into laughter and song at the most difficult times of his life. Like Francis, through acceptance and 'letting go', we too are able to laugh in spite of suffering and this is a sign of great hope. It is in this sense that Del Close, who, as the father of modern improvized humour, influenced such comedic greats as Bill Murray, John Belushi and Mike Myers, could regard spiritual truth and humour as intricately connected. 'Plainly put,' summarized Mike Myers, '"ha-ha" is related to "ah-ha".'

Laughter and resurrection

Despite the many virtues of laughter, we also have to recognize its limits and its potential for causing offence, hurt and pain. Humour, after all, can undoubtedly reflect escapism, cruelty, callousness or lack of involvement. Suffering especially can be met with thoughtless, wicked or cruel laughter. Christ himself was mocked with malicious laughter as he hung in agony on the cross. Laughter has, then, a dichotic potential – it can build-up or cast-down, it can be cynical or joyous, it can be manipulative or guileless. There is, for example, a huge difference between the laughter of the Nazi oppressors or white slave owners and the laughter of the Holocaust victims or the black slaves.

Similarly, even the most selfless laughter needs to be adapted to time, place and person. Unconsidered attempts to 'cheer up' a depressed, grieving or suffering person can have disastrous consequences. On the other hand, the American literary critic Anatole Broyard noted that during his own serious illness his witty and irreverent friends suddenly became intensely serious and solemn. 'They looked at me', he recalled, 'with a kind of grotesque lovingness in their faces.' Cheap jokes during someone's suffering can be insensitive and hurtful, but a lack of a profound sense of irony and humour revealed to Broyard that his friends, like Job's friends in the Old Testament, simply could not deal with his situation. Here we return to the crux of the issue – the concern that some things are simply beyond humour, and the worry that, through humour, we can end up trivializing life and death. Thus, theologians such as Reinhold Niebuhr urge tears of regret and transformation during suffering, rather than tears of joy. 'There is laughter in the vestibule of the temple, the echo of laughter in the temple itself,' wrote Niebuhr, 'but only faith and prayer, and no laughter, in the holy of holies.'

Interestingly, Niebuhr points to Nazi concentration camps as one place where only faith and prayer, and not laughter, would have had any impact. Yet here he seems to have ignored evidence from Auschwitz survivors, such as Frankl and Wiesel. Traditionally, Jewish humour does not minimize or avoid suffering, even in the most hopeless situations. Rather, Jewish humour embraces those distressing circumstances, and has therefore helped purge the depression and hopelessness that has threatened Jews in so many hostile circumstances. In fact, being Jewish and having a 'good sense of humour' has almost become synonymous, with a character in the hit US television sitcom *Seinfeld* presented as converting to the Jewish faith solely 'for the jokes'. In the face of diverse hardships, laughter has bound Jewish people together and helped them adapt to often hostile, changing circumstances. One telling and poignant joke was told among European Jews in the early 1940s and was later to be resurrected in Israel during the troubles in the 1970s:

A bishop, an imam, and a rabbi were debating what their people would do if the Almighty sent a second Great Flood.

'We would pray for forgiveness and salvation,' opines the bishop.

'We would accept our kismet and go to meet Allah,' replies the imam.

And the rabbi says, 'We would learn to live underwater.'

Victor Frankl suggests that such Jewish humour was one of the soul's principal 'weapons in the fight for self-preservation' during the Holocaust. Frankl even took it upon himself to 'train' some of his fellow prisoners to develop a sense of humour, so certain was he that it gave hope and meaning to lives. The claim that laughter is a spontaneous gift that cannot be programmed into our lives self-consciously needs, therefore, to be reassessed. A number of theologians and psychologists have subsequently agreed with Frankl, with laughter being described as a spiritual and emotional keep-fit technique, an inner jogging, that can be practised during times of both pleasure and pain.

Indeed, in his poem 'Lough Derg', Patrick Kavanagh describes resurrection as 'a laugh freed' for eternity. Just as Christ's resurrection can be seen as part of God's laughter, so laughter can help lead to our own resurrections. Through the light that laughter brings into our lives, moments of suffering can become moments of rebirth and freedom. Laughing at one's prison walls, then, is not desperate cynicism or self-deception, but is rather the first step to scaling those walls to new life and freedom.

6

Building blocks: memory

'God gave us memories that we might have roses in December'
J. M. Barrie

'We physicists believe the separation between past, present, and future is only an illusion, although a convincing one'
Albert Einstein

Introduction

'There are many ways to define our shallow existence, many ways to give it meaning,' muses the narrator in the hit TV show *Heroes*. That episode had shown the character Peter Petrelli desperately trying to remember his past after his memory had been erased. His friend, Adam Monroe, had persuaded him that healing could only take place through the recovery of his memory, which would occur when he concentrated on what mattered most to him. The narrator therefore concludes that memories hold the key to life's context and purpose. Memories are, he maintains, 'what separate us, what make us human, and, in the end, what we must fight to hold on to'.

As Christians, our worth is certainly not to be judged on our ability to retain or recall information and incidences. Memory, however, still has an important place in our Christian life and should have an intimate relationship with our sense of meaning and hope. In the fear, humiliation and anger of the concentration camp, Viktor Frankl claims that the very worst of human suffering was rendered tolerable by the memory of happier times. Past events, he claimed, gave prisoners refuge from the emptiness and desolation of their experiences. Interestingly, these events were 'often not important ones, but minor happenings and trifling things'. In some way, then, even our most fundamental memories allow us to step outside of time and space and to experience life's eternal dimension. As such, if we employ it in a positive manner, memory is one way in which we can begin to transcend our distress and suffering.

Memory and suffering

While humankind has made phenomenal breakthroughs in science and medicine over the past few centuries, neurologists still remain somewhat perplexed by human consciousness. Yet we create our individual worlds in reaction to our conscious and unconscious memories. Memories make us who we are and their power over us is substantial. This, of course, can be positive or else very damaging, as good and unhappy memories live in us side by side. Many lives are destroyed by painful memories, and much time and resources are employed in an attempt to facilitate the healing of such memories. Lives are also destroyed by an unhealthy attachment to happy memories. Memories, after all, can keep individuals, groups and even nations in bondage to the past.

In the context of unhappy memories, psychology and psychiatry have shown us that we are free to choose a different *past* and subsequently a different *future*. Less frequently recognized is the fact that more positive and happy memories can help us choose a different *present*. Like peeling an onion, we will find layers and layers of memories inside of us, and it can be so rewarding to spend time being nourished by those layers. When my grandfather visits, I have often found him sitting in the darkness in my living room. I once asked him why he did this and his answer was revealing. 'My knees are hurting, my hip has been replaced, I can't walk far without getting out of breath, and my wife and best friends are all dead, but I can still enjoy myself spending time with my memories,' he said with a smile on his face. Perhaps Philip Larkin's description of the elderly having lit rooms in their heads, with people acting in them, is less disparaging and negative than he intended.

The poet Grey Gowrie makes a more explicit link between memory and a temporary relief from life's hardships. In his poem 'Marches', written as he recovered from a heart transplant, he invites us to imagine beautiful woodland on the Welsh borders. Every day he transported himself from his bed in London to this place that was withheld from him by circumstances, and his detailed memory of the beauty of nature in that place eased his suffering. Pain, after all, makes us focus on our suffering, which Gowrie terms as 'pain's narrow horizon', and therefore excludes a wider vision. Memory offers us that wider vision.

There is, then, a deep reservoir of memories in all of us. Recent scientific research allows us to view these memories in a fresh way. Rather than regarding 'time' as flowing chronologically, many physicists regard events as simply existing in 'spacetime'. Thus, past, present and future are essentially meaningless, as all events are considered equally real. Furthermore, quantum physics holds that when two entities interact with each other, they can continue to influence each other, even when they are separated. Memory, then, is more than a mere recollection of experiences. It is, rather, a connection or dialogue with a past that still exists and continues to define us. Brian Keenan recalls how the memory of his father helped him survive his four-and-a-half-year ordeal as a hostage in Beirut. Despite being kept in isolation for two years, and being blindfolded and chained for much of the rest of the time, his memories brought him strength and comfort. 'My father became not just simply a memory but more a real presence,' he later wrote, 'a presence I could feel more than see, a comforting reassurance that eased the hurt into a deeply filled sadness, yet that same sadness as it became reflective, lifted me.'

Viktor Frankl relates the power of such uplifting memories to the timeless effect of love. In the senseless suffering of the concentration camp, he came to the conclusion that 'love is the ultimate and highest goal to which man can aspire . . . the salvation of man is through love and in love'. The memory of love shown to us in the past, therefore, allows that love to remain with us in the present, in spite of the most terrible suffering. He himself recalls the peace and fulfilment that a loving contemplation on the image of his beloved wife brought to him. Love, then, goes beyond the physical presence of a person, and, if we allow it, the memory of a loved person, whether living or dead, can be vivid and satisfying. 'More and more I felt that she was present, that she was with me,' he writes. 'I had the feeling that I was able to touch her, able to stretch out my hand and grasp hers. The feeling was very strong; she was *there*.'

God and memory

The concept of memory is paramount in scripture, not least because scripture is itself a record of the memory of God's people. As such, we are urged to remember the recorded actions of God in history, as well as remembering our personal experience of God's work in our lives. 'Be careful never to forget what you yourself have seen,' announces Deuteronomy 4.9; 'do not let these memories escape from your mind as long as you live' (NLT).

The Bible also asserts that God himself has a memory. In Genesis 8.21, after the flood and immediately before the rainbow is seen in the sky, God smells Noah's burnt offerings. Smell is a sense that evokes the past. It is, after all, the human sense with the longest 'memory'. By having God smell the offering at this point of the narrative, then, the writer of Genesis reminds us that God's memory is closely associated with his universal and eternal covenant with us. This tells us something profound about the nature of God – that he holds all time and space in his being as an eternal present.

For the early Israelites, this would have been the ultimate re-assurance. There was nothing worse for them than being forgotten. To be erased from God's memory was tantamount to never having existed. Later in the Old Testament, Isaiah reminds Israel that however much it seems as if God has abandoned them, he still remembers them everlastingly (Isa. 49.15). We can forget him but he eternally remembers us (cf. Luke 1.54). The past is, therefore, preserved and transformed in God. Our everyday experiences exist outside of space and time, and so each moment of our existence takes on permanent significance. Rather than being lost for ever, then, the past is timeless and eternal and can be accessed in the present to bring us hope, peace and joy.

Some theologians, such as A. N. Whitehead and John Polkinghorne, use this concept of 'divine remembrance' to explain life after death. Even after our passing, God everlastingly remembers us and, as God is in us and around us, the dead reside permanently in our memory, outside of time and space. 'We meet the living dead,' writes Karl Rahner, 'in faith, hope, and love, when we open our hearts to the silent calm of God's own self, in which they live.'

Through the death of a loved one, then, we are left with difficult and painful memories. But, in time, we can learn to search and celebrate memories of happy times shared. After all, death does not destroy the reality of relationships. Through divine remembrance, which underlies our own memories, our loved ones are present and accessible to us continually. In the Latin American base communities, for example, the names of the dead are read out aloud, with worshippers responding with '*presente*'. Likewise, in the Celtic tradition the veil between our world and the eternal world is regarded as thin. Dead loved ones, then, remain in our lives as an ongoing presence, as their memory lives on and transforms us. This fact is reflected in a number of films, as the dead hero appears on the screen towards the end of the film to show his or her continuing presence. In the classic film *Cool Hand Luke* (1967), for example, Paul Newman's character is persecuted, shot and killed by the corrupt guards in a US prison. The final scene sees his fellow inmates, gathering around to share stories and anecdotes about him. As this takes place, the audience is shown a montage of moments when he brought hope and joy to a place of despair and dejection.

Through our vivid memories, then, people we love who have died often have greater vitality to us than do the living. It therefore follows that memory is important in funerals, as we gather to recall how a person has touched our individual or corporate lives. Furthermore, memory is the basis of most of our rituals as humans, such as birthdays and anniversaries. In the Christian tradition, the principal ritual of the majority of mainstream denominations, that of the eucharist service, also has memory at its centre. 'Do this in remembrance if me,' was Christ's command at the Last Supper. The Greek word used for remembrance, *anamnesis*, implies much more than a mere recalling of an event from the distant past. Rather, it is the re-enactment of the past in the present, which itself influences the future. We gather around the altar to share in the memory of Christ's suffering and resurrection, but in doing so we bring the past to life and integrate it into our present experience.

The text, symbols and gestures used in our worship further trigger our memories. After all, they have identifiable messages and meanings and are an important part of our spiritual inheritance. Through the eucharist, we not only remember Christ himself, but also the faith of our forefathers and mothers who re-enacted this very same ceremony. As such, it can take us back very directly to years gone by and, for many of us, to our childhood. Those of us who take home communion to the elderly and infirm will know that the very words of the service become a cathartic catalyst for long-forgotten memories of the past. In my first ministerial appointment, I would regularly visit residents in a home for the elderly. One lady was particularly unfriendly to the nursing staff and to her fellow residents. Although raised a regular church attendee, she had not stepped foot in church for many decades and she made her distaste for prayer or holy communion abundantly clear. Still, she wanted me to sit with her each time I visited. One such time, lunch was brought to her bedside, and she immediately made known her unhappiness at that day's menu by pushing the tray off her lap. The poor care worker bent down to clear the floor of the discarded food, but was met with a barrage of abuse. This diatribe finished with a line that she must have drawn from a distant memory of her church-attending past – 'You, woman,' she screamed, 'are not worthy to gather up the crumbs under my table.' I proceeded to complete the phrase, from the 1662 Book of Common Prayer eucharistic service: 'but thou art the same Lord, whose property is always to have mercy'. We then sat in silence for five minutes, before she spoke. 'Vicar,' she said, having clearly reflected on how those words brought memories of happier times in her life, 'I think I'd like communion next time you visit.' In the succeeding six months, during which she suffered and died, I regularly visited that lady to give her communion. How the power of memory and eucharist can combine in our search for hope and meaning is, for me, summarized in the strength to face suffering that this individual gleaned from my weekly sojourns. 'I'm still not sure if I even believe in this God of yours,' she whispered to me from her hospital death bed, 'but I believe in the power of his body and blood.'

Awareness and memory

Each of us, then, however seemingly eventless our lives, has a deep well of memories, ready for us to trawl. 'I realized that a man who'd only lived for a day could easily live for a hundred years in a prison,' wrote Albert Camus in *The Outsider*, 'he'd have enough memories not to get bored.' Our memories can certainly hurt us, but they can also heal and give us hope. They can keep us firmly in bondage to the past, but they can also be used to root us in the present moment and look with hope to the future. For us to recognize which memories are good and also to notice when we become unhealthily dependent on good or bad memories, we need to employ awareness.

Paradoxically, our memory of the past should not rob the present moment of its reality. To glean from the past and look to the future, we need to be rooted firmly in an awareness of the present. However comforting it may seem to us, if we live blindly in the world of our memories, at the expense of the present, then we will fail to transcend external circumstances. Viktor Frankl, who championed memory as a way to grow beyond our suffering, nevertheless noticed that those Auschwitz prisoners who resided solely in the past had already lost their hope. 'Life for such people became meaningless,' he concluded.

By ensuring that our past does not become an idol, but by nevertheless becoming attentive to our memories in the present moment, we come to appreciate that God is not *in* memory but, rather, God comes *through* memory. This realization leads us to recognize God's work in our lives in the past, to become aware of

God in the present, and to long for a future with God. Our memory is, therefore, not a thing in itself, but is part of our relationship with God, which will be brought to fullness in the future. In other words, memories are, in the words of C. S. Lewis, 'only the scent of a flower we have not found; the echo of a tune we have not heard, news from a country we have never yet visited'.

Rather than taking us away from the present, then, our memories should help us throw new light on our circumstances and thus help us to look towards and transform the future. Memory, after all, is a form of presence, with the degree of that presence dependent on how aware we are of our experiences and our relationships. From my own teaching experience, I know that a student who has recently fallen in love will be more 'present' to his girlfriend, who may be many miles away, than he will be to me as his lecturer, who is standing right in front of him! To allow our memories to give hope and meaning to our lives, then, we need to be truly present to them – attentively, lovingly, and non-judgementally present to them. 'The past is never dead,' wrote William Faulkner in *Intruder in the Dust*; 'it is not even past.'

Storehouse of memories

Memory is the one signal of transcendence that relates directly to all the other building blocks in our temple of hope and meaning. Our memories of the beauty of nature and art, of laughter and of other people are often the most lasting and resonant. This is borne out both in academic research and in anecdotal evidence. Philip Yancey, for example, describes a 'farewell' tour his friend undertook. She was diagnosed with a condition that would leave her blind and so doctors suggested she should revisit her favourite places so they would live on in her memory when darkness descended. Yancey, who himself relates beauty in nature to God's presence, described this as 'storing away a memory bank of grace'. Other commentators have used other poetic phrases to describe our storehouse of memories – a 'necklace of experience', a 'soul's art gallery', 'the beads of life', 'the temple of memory' and a 'room called remember'.

Perhaps this is something of what Jesus meant when he called us to invest in what he called 'the good treasure of the heart' (Luke 6.45), and we certainly don't need tragedy to beset us before we begin to consciously store away good memories, to be brought out and savoured in moments of need. Each day we need to ask ourselves what new memories we have made. The secret of making such memories is, of course, awareness of the present moment. 'The true art of memory,' wrote Samuel Johnson, 'is the art of attention.' Once the memories have been made, however, they then need to be harvested, so they become food for our soul. We should, in a sense, put ourselves in the position of the disciples on the road to Emmaus, as we take any opportunity to remember the presence of Jesus, through signals of transcendence in our lives. Especially in our times of suffering, memories can slip away from us. They are wonderful, but they are also elusive. It is certainly difficult to discover gold in our memories, with no rainbow in sight. Still during those dark times, remembered grace can bring light into our lives, which can help us from getting stuck in reactivity and can give us new perspective on situations. It is, therefore, important that we practise remembering, so that we root ourselves in memories of God's loving kindness. These are the 'Precious Memories' of the traditional gospel hymn, covered by Bob Dylan and Johnny Cash among others – the 'sacred scenes' that linger in our subconscious. We can, of course, harvest such memories through a plethora of techniques, each one of which benefits different personalities and temperaments. These techniques include silence (the 'stillness of midnight', as the above hymn puts it), prayer, poems, letters, song, dance, meditation, pilgrimage, visits to gravesides, worship, the eucharist, visits to childhood places, visits to people, art, nature, and so on.

Indeed, when his fellow prisoners had reached their lowest ebb, Frankl encouraged such a harvesting of memories for comfort. The past, he maintained, could bring light into the darkness they faced. 'What you have experienced,' he wrote, 'no power on earth can take from you.' Our memories, after all, are eternal and sacred, and so by looking backwards, we are, in some paradoxical way, also looking forwards in hope. For C. S. Lewis, a toy garden that his brother had made brought this fact alive. He described the garden as 'the first beauty I ever knew', as it made him aware of nature as 'something cool, dewy, fresh, exuberant'. The event itself, however, became far less significant to him than the memory of that moment. After all, his memory of that rather insignificant toy garden pointed to a future without suffering, worry and pain. And so, in that 'memory of a memory', was both paradise lost and paradise regained. 'As long as I live,' he concluded, 'my imagination of Paradise will retain something of my brother's toy garden.'

7

Building blocks: art

—•◆•—

'A man should hear a little music, read a little poetry, and see a fine picture every day of his life, in order that worldly cares may not obliterate the sense of the beautiful which God has implanted in the human soul'   *Johann Wolfgang von Goethe*

'When writers make us shake our heads with the exactness of their prose and their truths, and even make us laugh about ourselves or life, our buoyancy is restored . . . You can't stop the raging storm, but singing can change the hearts and spirits of the people who are together on that ship'   *Anne Lamott*

Introduction

At the end of the film adaptation of Ian McEwan's *Atonement* (2007), the character Bryony Tiller reveals herself to be the writer of the story and confesses to having changed true-life events to give the readers of her book a 'sense of hope or satisfaction'. The story had hinged on an incident when she had falsely accused her sister's lover of rape. In her book she had described how, later in life, her sister had been happily reunited with her lover. Bryony now confesses that no happy ending actually took place, as Robbie had died on a beach at Dunkirk and Cecilia had been killed during the London blitz. 'In the book I wanted to give Robbie and Cecilia what they lost out on in life,' Bryony muses. 'I'd like to think this isn't weakness or evasion, but a final act of kindness.' Thus, she believed that the book had given to the doomed couple, and, as a result, to the reader, a fulfilment and happiness that real life had not offered. Whether or not we believe that Bryony atoned for her deceit by offering this new vision of reality, few of us would deny that despite the tragedies that beset us, art offers the potential to lift our hearts and bring hope into otherwise hopeless situations.

Viktor Frankl surprisingly claims to have experienced the 'beauty of art' as never before during his Holocaust ordeal. He recalls with fondness, for example, the cabaret that the prisoners would occasionally improvize. Temporarily, a hut would be cleared and wooden benches pushed together to form a makeshift stage. The prisoners then gathered there 'to have a few laughs or perhaps cry a little; anyway, to forget'. They would even forgo their daily portion of food to attend the cabaret, and their hearts would be lifted as they enjoyed songs, jokes, satires and poems. 'All were meant to help us forget,' he concludes, 'and they did help.'

Suffering is chaotic and disorientating. Art, on the other hand, is rooted in order and beauty, and, as such, naturally offers relief from our afflictions. In fact, evidence suggests that, rather than waning during suffering, our sensitivity to and appreciation of the arts actually heightens. As a young man, John Stuart Mill noted that music alone was able to lift him out of gloom, despair and depression. In the depth of suffering, the arts can certainly touch the core of our being. It is, therefore, little surprise that to many of us, even if we are nominal Christians or non-believers, the most moving part of a funeral are the hymns, music, readings or poetry. Paradoxically, they make us experience grief and pain more intensely, while bringing consolation and solace at the same time.

Rarely can we adequately put our suffering into words. Art either does this for us, in the form of literature, poetry, song-lyrics and films, or it expresses the wordlessness of emotions, through music or paintings. As such, artistic expression has the ability to touch people at times of both individual crisis and collective distress. In the US after the tragic events of 9/11, for example, the media spotlighted how art was being employed by ordinary people to face the turmoil. In dealing with the complex emotions of grief and trauma, many spontaneously turned to creating artworks or writing songs. The more famous art and songs (such as Alan Jackson's country hit 'Where Were You When the World Stopped Turning (that September day)?') were the tip of the iceberg of the creativity that poured out following the tragedy. As such, when we face even the most dreadful circumstances, in the words of Nietzsche, 'art approaches as a saving sorceress, expert at healing. She alone knows how to turn these nauseous thoughts about the horror or absurdity of existence into notions with which one can live.'

Art and hope

Our propensity to enjoy the arts is manifest in every past society and present culture, and shows itself in our very early years. It lies deep within the core of our human nature. Yet, the arts have stumped evolutionists, with Darwin referring to the enjoyment of music as, biologically, one of the 'faculties of the least use to man' and Stephen Pinker referring to music as 'auditory cheese-cake'. Most of the arts, continues Pinker, are biologically useless and could therefore disappear from our species without affecting the rest of our lifestyles to a great extent.

Yet, few of us would deny the importance of art in our everyday lives. Art and happiness, for example, are inextricably linked, as often our passion for the arts goes hand in hand with our appreciation of life. Darwin himself admitted that when his love for music and poetry waned, his intellect, his emotions and, most of all, his sense of joy at the gift of life were impaired. Art, of course, also acts as a healer once unhappiness has broken through into our lives. After all, art is profoundly emotional and can pierce our hearts directly, requiring no mediation other than itself. Art can comfort us, calm us, inspire us and animate us. It can stimulate our feelings, our creativity, our sense of humour and our imagination.

Although often challenging and thought-provoking, then, art is also, as the mission statement of the American Art Therapy Association asserts, healing and life-enhancing. An artistic creation is a gift from an artist, and it holds the potential to revive our souls in so many different ways. It has long been accepted that art can stimulate or enhance various cognitive abilities in children. Yet, scientific evidence is now also showing us that the arts can have a profoundly positive effect on physical, psychological and emotional illnesses. Extensive research, for example, has revealed the positive effects of the arts on those suffering from Parkinson's, bipolar disorder, dementia, depression and many other conditions.

The effectiveness of art as a healer and comforter does not even require us to have any formal knowledge of specific art forms. We do not, for example, have to be particularly 'musical' to respond to music at the deepest level of our psyche. Similarly, art does not have to be complex to affect us profoundly. 'The simpler the image, the vaster the dream,' writes the French philosopher Gaston Bachelard. Neither does art have to be highbrow to have an impact on us. The simple and popular arts of everyday life, such as pop music and blockbuster films, can be as effective a healer as loftier, more complex forms of art. Young people, especially, regard popular culture as an important medium and resource for meaning and comfort. Thus, television, film, pop music and video games should not be dismissed in our quest to find seeds of hope in the dark soil of our suffering. After all, both high and low arts are, paradoxically, both a parallel of our own lives and relationships and, in the words of poet Seamus Heaney, 'a glimpsed alternative' of them. Thus, they affirm us to accept our lives as they are and they offer us the hope that situations can be redeemed and transformed.

Art and faith

Both the Old and the New Testaments begin with creative acts of love that have ultimate implications for art and artists. The gift of creation at the beginning of the Old Testament describes God imposing order out of chaos. Before giving the earth to humanity for its enjoyment and delight, God looks at what he has formed and 'He saw that it was good', a phrase repeated more than any other in the creation accounts. Likewise, human creative artists wrestle with raw materials, whether paint, stone, music or language,

77

and imposes order upon them. We, the viewer and the listener, then look upon the created art and we see that it is good.

With the incarnation in the New Testament, God personally becomes involved in our everyday struggles. When artists explore the discord and lack of order in the world, we are reminded that, in the person of Christ, God himself both experienced and overcame our fallen world. Thus, through the resurrected Christ's continued presence to us in the created order, the whole of life becomes sacramental, and art reflects this. As Eric Gill stated: 'What is a work of art? A word made flesh.'

The theme of the goodness of creativity and the arts is, then, biblical at its core. Yet, faith and art have not always collaborated in a mutually acceptable manner. There have been times in history when religious intolerance, piety or sentimentality has threatened the human creative spirit. Rather than making life rich in colour and creativity, Christianity has often made the material world dark, bland and dismal. The long-standing tradition of duality in Christian thinking is at the root of this unfortunate situation, with traditional teaching regarding the spiritual as good and the material as evil. Thus, the Christian life becomes compartmentalized, with the arts being seen as secondary to lofty spiritual ideals. When the poet Wilfred Owen was killed on the fields of France, just a week before the end of the First World War, a draft of a letter to his local vicar was found among his possessions. In it, he criticizes his boyhood faith for having no proper place for the aesthetic. It was, he claimed, anti-body, anti-beauty and anti-art. A later poet, the Welsh clergyman R. S. Thomas, vividly described the Protestant faith especially as 'the adroit castrator of art' and 'the bitter negation of song and dance and the heart's innocent joy'.

Such a hostile attitude of the Church towards art, however, is a terrible distortion of what Christianity should be. In the King James version of the Bible, the Greek words *sarx* and *pneuma*, which are starkly contrasted in Paul's letters, are translated as 'flesh' and 'spirit'. Thus, for most of Christian history, flesh and spirit have, indeed, been regarded as polar opposites, continually struggling against each other. In fact, instead of a simple material/non-material dichotomy, Paul's description is actually of the struggle between an existence organized against God and an existence shaped by God. In the latter, we become at one with God. Beauty, creativity and art, then, are not to be placed within Paul's description of *sarx*. Rather, they are to be placed within the context of the creation and incarnation, and, therefore, to be regarded as a direct, good and gracious gift from God to his children.

This innate material goodness is certainly not exclusive to the creativity of believers, as even St Paul recognized the value of Greek culture. He, therefore, would not have expected us to expose ourselves to the ideas and thoughts of fellow Christians alone. Furthermore, art itself is universal. It deals with the human condition and the world around us, and there is nothing that it should shy away from. All works of art, then, whatever their subject matter and whatever the artist's faith or lack of faith, are reflections of the conviction that God created us to become co-creators with him, fashioning order out of chaos. 'Everything,' wrote the French impressionist painter Edgar Degas, 'everything in this world has a sacred meaning.'

Art and faith, then, are intricately related. Paul Tillich suggested that this is because both are concerned with the expression of ultimate reality. Many Christians, he maintained, see their faith as driven by rigid concepts, subjective emotions and moral laws. By doing so, however, they fail to recognize the 'numinous power' that can be found in people, symbols, words and acts. The arts are rooted in this power. As such, they open levels of mystery and reality in the ordinary that would otherwise be hidden. There is even some scientific evidence for this, as the neurological origin of artistic, mystical and religious feelings are closely inter-related.

Even many religious sceptics recognize that art holds a power that points to something beyond itself. The BBC Radio 4 programme *Devout Sceptics* saw numerous avowed atheists and agnostics relating their love of the arts in near-religious terms. The jazz musician George Melly asserted that he 'felt awe, and very religious awe, in front of certain paintings', the writer Jeanette Winterson spoke of 'connecting to something much bigger than you' in literature, and the actress Sheila Hancock claimed she was 'moved, comforted, and delighted' by music, 'just as moved as I would be by a religious service – because it is living proof'. On reflecting on this trend, the presenter Bel Mooney asserted that she was certain that art leads 'agnostics like myself to tiptoe towards the deity'.

Through art, then, we sense, and then respond to, something of the Beyond. By taking our ordinary, everyday experiences, and pointing to something that is beyond them, art gives us an intense experience of 'otherness'. Thus, the beauty, form, order and ineffable quality of art allows us to experience transcendence. It is, however, important that we do not allow our creations to become our God. The wonder of art is, after all, also in its expression of the world's pain, ugliness and evil. Art reminds us that the transcendent is both here *and* not here. It is, then, not *in* art that we glean hope, but *through* art. Art is not God, as to regard art as divine would be idolatrous. But the transcendent does live in our creativity and he uses it to transform our lives.

In the introduction to a collection of his lyrics, the rock musician Nick Cave suggests that art, suffering and God are all, in fact, inextricably linked. The transcendent eases our troubles and soothes the depths of our being, when, for example, we compose or listen to music. 'The love song,' Cave writes, 'is the light of God, deep down, blasting through our wounds.' He cites Psalm 137 (later turned by Boney M into a chart hit entitled 'By the Rivers of Babylon') and Kylie Minogue's 'Better the Devil You Know' as two examples of how art can help alleviate our suffering by bridging the yawning chasm that pain places between God and ourselves. Therefore, artists, like Cave himself, with his dark and angst-ridden compositions, act as soothing, spiritual balm for a troubled world:

> Me, I'm a soul-catcher for God. Here I come with my butterfly-net of words. Here I catch the chrysalis. Here I blow life into bodies and hurl them fluttering to the stars and the care of God.

Art and awareness

Stravinsky suggested that, in the midst of the creative process, all artists must remain steadfastly in the present moment. Likewise, when listening to a piece of music, contemplating a painting or watching a film, we must also root ourselves in the present, and not be bound to the past or blinded by the future. Sometimes we even become as one with the artist in a continuing present moment. In landscape paintings, for example, we contemplate in our here-and-now the scene the artist was witnessing in his or her here-and-now. As such, we are drawn into his or her present moment. To assist us in our journey, artists will often place a figure at the forefront of the painting, looking out on the landscape. This figure is often inconspicuous and subtle, but can sometimes be obvious and imposing, as in many paintings of Caspar David Friedrich. We, therefore, become the contemporary eyes of these figures, blessed to relive their present moment as often as we desire.

In light of its close relationship with the present moment, then, it is only natural that art often interacts with the other 'building blocks' that we have rooted in awareness. Art can make us laugh, it can help inspire altruism, and, especially through painting, photography and film, it can bring us closer to the natural world. Furthermore, through the work of a human creator our senses can be left open and eager to appreciate more fully the work of the Creator in the other 'building blocks'. If, for example, we go for a walk in the countryside after we have visited a gallery of landscape paintings, we can find that we notice shapes and colours we had hitherto missed or taken for granted.

The 'building block' with the closest affiliation to art, however, is memory. After all, art lives on in our memory long after our direct experience of its forms is over. Researchers in the 1960s carried out experiments that became known as 'the White Christmas effect'. So powerful is our memory of music that subjects even claimed to hear Bing Crosby sing when experimenters announced that they were playing the song at a low volume, but did not actually turn it on. Our memories can certainly fire and inspire visual and musical imagery. 'Heard melodies are sweet, but those unheard are sweeter,' wrote John Keats in 'Ode on a Grecian Urn'. The most extraordinary example of this is, of course, Beethoven, who continued to be moved by music, and to compose music, long after he lost his hearing.

Art can also act as a can-opener for our memories. We even talk about a 'soundtrack to our lives', as we recall the tunes of our past and relate them to specific events and the emotions associated with those events. The country-music group Alabama sang of a jukebox in the corner of our minds that continually plays our 'favourite memories'. It is, therefore, only natural that art therapy, especially in the form of music and paintings, is used to bring fulfilment, joy and pleasure to those suffering the degenerative process of dementia. After all, a person with Alzheimer's may lose a number of fundamental aspects of self-awareness, but a recollection of the arts is frequently preserved, even at very advanced stages of the disease. I witnessed this fact during regular visits to minister to sufferers of dementia and Alzheimer's in a home for the elderly in South Wales. I would lead services there and frequently noticed patients 'come to life', as it were, during the hymn-singing. On one occasion, an elderly man, who was in quite a late stage of dementia, stood up at the end of a service and sang a word-perfect solo for us. The parts of the service in the Welsh language had clearly triggered memories that seemed to have been long lost. The Welsh hymn 'Pantyfedwen' tripped off his tongue as smoothly as a child reciting times tables, and the words were poignant and striking:

> Rwyf heddiw'n gweld yr harddwch sy'n parhau
> Rwy'n teimlo'r ddwyfol ias sy'n bywiocau;
> Mae'r Haleliwia yn fy enaid i
> A rhoddaf, Iesu, fy mawrhâd i Ti.

> (I see the beauty now that can survive,
> I feel the touch divine that makes alive;
> The Hallelujah has possessed my soul,
> To You, O! Christ, I give my praises all.)

The power of music and poetry seemed to return something of this man that had seemed irretrievably lost, and the process served also to trigger a sense of transcendence. As he sat back down, he held his heart and muttered: 'You see, He's still with me; I thought He'd gone, but He's still with me.'

Art, then, is created in a point of history and belongs to a certain time and a place. But when we recall a melody and we play it in our mind, it becomes newly alive. We are, in a sense, re-creating it in our own time and place. Thus, the past becomes very much the present moment. This goes some way to explaining how, even when we have listened to a piece of music or looked at a painting many times, it can seem as fresh and new as the first time we heard or saw it. Viktor Zuckerkandl, the Austrian musicologist, points to performing musicians as a supreme example of this. Their ultimate sign of success is if they are able to play a familiar piece as if it were being heard by an audience for the first time. This truly is, he claims, 'the creation of the present moment'.

Engaging with art

Engaging with the arts can certainly be a very practical way of dealing with suffering. On one hand, the arts can help us cathartically to focus on our troubles. Aristotle described theatre as a cathartic exercise for the troubled mind. Many of the arts today can play the same role. We absorb ourselves in them, relate them to our own experiences, and vicariously work out our emotions and feelings through them. They, therefore, give order and clarity to situations, and can help us view our circumstances in new and different ways. Through them, we see beyond the ordinary, as we encounter new entrances into reality. When we penetrate deep into our darkness through art, we can emerge into the light of real life with refreshed hope.

Conversely, on the other hand, art can distract us and take us briefly away from our troubles. This can give us valuable time and space away from the worries and concerns that are racing around our minds. When we place ourselves in the presence of the beauty of art, we somehow become that beautiful thing and it works a mystery and a magic in us that can heal and sustain. In this sense, art can become, as novelist Amy Tan has described, a form of prayer or meditation.

Silent contemplation on art is certainly one natural and powerful way of engagement. In such a practice, we do not need to 'think' about, or try to 'understand', anything. There is certainly a time and place for hermeneutics and interpretation, but discovering mystery, beauty and transcendence can begin with simply immersing ourselves in the present moment in the presence of a creation. Schumann is said to have finished playing a newly composed piece to a friend, who, puzzled by the composition, asked what it actually meant. 'It means this,' replied Schumann, and he played it again. Meaning, then, is of secondary importance to how an artwork affects us. So, in the process of silent contemplation on art, we need to instruct ourselves mentally to forget our 'feelings' about it. Rather, we simply let it work its effect. In a sense, that is 'letting God speak'. We look or listen with open attentiveness and awareness, allowing the creation to soothe our emotions. Such aesthetic contemplation can bring great rewards, but, like meditation itself, it is a discipline that is enhanced through regular practice.

In such contemplation, there is certainly a wide range of art to be explored – paintings, musical compositions, dance, film, architecture, and so on. Each and every art form can bring a new shade of colour to the bleakness of our suffering. The playful and humorous component in art is certainly important. John Stuart Mill, for example, championed the effect of cheerful music on his emotions. It is, however, not only happy and joyful art that can have a profound effect on our suffering, but also, paradoxically, melancholic and sad pieces of art. These can release pain or grief and allow emotions to flow again. We must, however, ensure that we do not allow ourselves to dwell unhealthily in such bleak art, which can allow us to feed our sadness and, worse still, to perversely enjoy doing so.

The power of art, then, is multi-faceted and can touch the body, soul and emotions of an individual. Yet, its healing gift to us cannot be forced. It, rather, comes to us as a blessing. 'The arts are not drugs,' wrote E. M. Forster; 'they are not guaranteed to act when taken.' This does not mean that listening, watching and looking are, therefore, purely passive functions. We need to maintain a positive and proactive role in our engagement with art, not least by taking steps to put ourselves in the presence of the kind of art that we know affects us. As we listen to a piece of music, look at a painting or watch a film, we also need to actively bring our attention to the process, alongside a willingness to engage with the potentially transforming experience it offers. Some of us will prefer an even more active engagement with the arts – playing music, painting, taking photographs, flower-arranging, and so on. In our own artistic activities, then, we can help contain the chaos and express the struggle of our suffering. Art will certainly not rid the world of suffering and wounds, but it can help transform them. After all, art carries energy, vitality, creativity and healing medicines that nourish, balm and restore our hearts and souls. 'I now see that sorrow, being the supreme emotion of which man is capable,' wrote Oscar Wilde from prison, 'is at once the type and test of all great art.' At the root of the change and transformation that the arts bring, then, is the fact that they are imbued with a sense of transcendence. In sentiments that echo Paul Tillich's description of God as 'the ground of being', Virginia Woolf described how the arts engender in us 'moments of being' and this, in some way, unites us with the very ground of existence. 'It is a constant idea of mine,' she concluded, 'that behind the cotton wool is hidden a pattern, that we – I mean all human beings – are connected with this, that the whole world is a work of art . . . We are the words. We are the music. We are the thing itself.'

8

Building blocks: helping others

———•◦•———

'I don't know what your destiny will be, but one thing I know: the only ones among you who will be really happy are those who will have sought and found how to serve'   *Albert Schweitzer*

'You will find that the mere resolve not to be useless, and the honest desire to help other people, will, in the quickest and delicatest ways, improve yourself'   *John Ruskin*

Introduction

In the book *Tuesdays with Morrie*, later turned into a film with Jack Lemmon and Hank Azaria, Mitch Albom describes the last few months in the life of his former college professor, Morrie Schwartz. As motor neurone disease ravages Morrie's body, Mitch regularly visits him and their old friendship is rekindled. During this time, Mitch is struck by his elderly mentor's attitude to suffering and impending death. Instead of retreating into melancholy and anxiety, Morrie squeezes every ounce of hope and meaning from the brief time he has left. Most of all, Mitch is struck by the difference between his own selfish individualism and Morrie's increasing desire to connect with others. 'I had become too wrapped up in the siren song of my own life,' muses Mitch Albom, 'I was busy.' Conversely, despite increasing pain and incapacity, Morrie continues to thrive off his interaction with others. 'The way you get meaning into your life is to devote yourself to loving others,' he told his former student; 'devote yourself to your community around you.' Yet, despite the fact that self-centredness was failing to bring him fulfilment, Mitch continued to question this logic, suggesting that we have too much pain and suffering in our own lives to waste time worrying about others. 'But giving to other people is what makes me feel alive . . .', answered Morrie, only weeks before his death, 'when I give my time, when I can make someone smile after they were feeling sad, it's as close to healthy as I ever feel.'

In facing our suffering, then, we have two choices. We can choose to allow our circumstances to push us towards the kind of unhealthy navel-gazing that leads to self-obsession. This is a lonely path that almost always results in resentfulness and bitterness. Alternatively, we can take the opportunity to grow outwards, towards, not only an awareness of life's joys, but also an empathy for others who suffer. Meaning and hope is, therefore, found in the benevolent circle that suffering can inspire. Love is offered to us when we suffer, and we, in turn, offer love to others who are facing difficult circumstances. In many ways, this echoes the basic principles of the ethics of gift exchange, where gifts are circulated without expectation of reward or payment. Similarly, our good deeds are carried out freely, but each one naturally leads to another. We 'pay it forward', as the film of that name put it. This principle serves to enliven and bring hope to individuals, communities and society. 'If money goes, money comes,' claimed Dr Aziz in E. M. Forster's *A Passage to India*; 'if money stays, death comes.' Thus, like ripples on a pond, our good deeds will have far-reaching effects on far more people than we realize.

Suffering and helping others

Viktor Frankl made a conscious decision during the Holocaust that he would spend time and effort helping his fellow prisoners. Rather than doing so out of a sense of duty or sacrifice, he did so to reassure himself that there was purpose and meaning in the senselessness of the concentration camp. As a result, he made use of his pre-Holocaust training by volunteering for medical duties. Thus, facing suffering required not only a certain frame of mind and way of thinking, but also, in his words, 'right action' and 'right conduct'. At the same time as Frankl was incarcerated in Europe,

British Army Officer Ernest Gordon was coming to similar conclusions in the Prisoner of War camps of the Far East. Forced, in awful conditions, to help construct the Burma–Siam railway, he considered altruistic relationship as the only way the prisoners could face the hell they were enduring with dignity and hope. 'Selfishness, hatred, envy, jealousy, greed, self-indulgence, laziness and pride were all anti-life,' he later concluded; 'love, heroism, self-sacrifice, sympathy, mercy, integrity and creative faith, on the other hand, were the essence of life, turning mere existence into living in its truest sense.'

The impact and influence of our behaviour certainly has far-reaching implications, not only for those whose lives we touch, but also on our own sense of purpose. We, in a sense, *create* meaning in our lives through our generosity in helping others. In the face of the meaninglessness of suffering, we can choose to bless, rather than curse. By doing so, our love and empathy forge hope and meaning and we return balance to life's equilibrium.

During our suffering, then, however much we are held captive by our own thoughts and worries, it is important to remind ourselves that there *is* a world outside of us. Life, after all, is not all about 'me'. Many of the tourists who survived the tsunami of Boxing Day 2004 recall how lovingly and selflessly the Thai people, who themselves had lost friends and relatives, cared for them. In suffering, we can make that choice to strengthen our inner ethics and we can begin to look outwards at the world that suffers alongside us. After all, one element of overcoming our pain and depression is to spend time devoting ourselves to others. By moving away from a focus on our own particular afflictions, we paradoxically ease that suffering. When Mother Teresa was asked what we should do to feel better about ourselves, she answered that we should go out and help somebody less fortunate, as 'it does wonders for the soul'.

Indeed, sometimes our suffering only makes any sense because of what it contributes to other people. After all, when we have experienced any form of tragedy and pain, we can begin to empathize with others who are going through difficulties. Learning from our negative experiences, we can use what we have gleaned to help others in their situations, as we reach out in love to those who remain in darkness. 'Let us rather be thankful,' wrote George Eliot in *Adam Bede*, 'that our sorrow lives in us as an indestructible source, only changing its form, as forces do, and passing from pain into sympathy – the one poor word which includes our best insights and our best love.'

Benefits of helping others

Isolation is one of the most destructive influences on our physical and mental health. Research has shown that those of us who have good social support during a time of crisis have a hastier and more lasting recovery than those who suffer alone. To find meaning and hope in our suffering we, therefore, need to escape from our tendency to turn to isolating activities during our times of trial. However much we think we enjoy excessive amounts of time on our own, as we work, travel, exercise or immerse ourselves in digital technology, we remain, at our very core, social creatures. We thrive off companionship, mutual respect and cooperation. As such, all of us need reassurance that we are not alone in our suffering, and, likewise, we need to reassure others that they are not alone in theirs.

Even our survival as a race can be attributed to our ability to support each other and our desire to work together. Despite our suffering, most of our lives are far from being, as Thomas Hobbes put it, 'solitary, poor, nasty, brutish and short', but are full of colour, cooperation and compassion. Research shows that by the age of two many children will have already developed the capacity to give basic comfort, by patting and hugging family members and other children who are hurt. It seems that our altruistic tendencies are deep-rooted in our genes, which goes some way to explaining how they bring a direct satisfaction to us. Whereas Immanuel Kant claimed that 'doing the right thing' should not be pleasurable, the MRI scanner shows that good deeds do actually bring us much fulfilment and happiness. In fact, their physiological effect on our brains is similar to when we take pleasure-enhancing drugs. Furthermore, research shows that those of us with a strong moral and social sense are mentally and physically healthier, and even do better socially and economically, than those who lack inter-personal moral sensibilities.

Cooperation, relationship and harmony, then, bring reward to us as both communities and individuals. According to sociologists, we accumulate 'social capital' in our everyday lives, which we store up in our 'social bank accounts'. Such social capital is earned through good personal relationships, community spirit and social cohesion. Research shows that those with healthy social capital have fewer mental health issues, recover more quickly from illness, and ultimately live longer and more fulfilling lives.

Despite this, the evidence also suggests that there has been a general decline in social capital in recent years, largely due to the contemporary social trend towards individualism. The cultivating of an outward focus in life is becoming rare in our society. In 2001 a government survey showed that only 32 per cent of British adults are involved in voluntary work, with young people the least likely to be engaged in local community projects and outreach. Yet, many sociologists and philosophers now believe that increasing happiness in our lives is very much related to the waning of our self-absorption. The Harvard Study of Adult Development, generally regarded as the finest study of twentieth-century lifestyles, found that 'personally satisfying altruism' is one of the principal hallmarks of a healthy and fulfilled life.

By transcending the self, then, we are taken away from continually dwelling on our own feelings and brooding on our own circumstances. When we give time to other people, our own selfish wants and needs become secondary. Rather than asking what we want from life, perhaps we should be asking what life wants from us. Ironically, by doing so, we may well find that the very fulfilment and purpose that we are searching for in our own lives follows. 'It is one of the beautiful compensations of life,' claimed the nineteenth-century philosopher Ralph Waldo Emerson, 'that no man can sincerely try to help another without helping himself.'

Helping others and our faith

Compassion, empathy and kindness are central themes throughout the Bible. The Old Testament is insistent that our good deeds will be repaid by reward, while doing evil will be punished. 'Do what is right and good in the LORD's sight,' asserts Deuteronomy 6.18, 'so that it may go well with you.' Our own experience of life, however, shows that reward is very often not the consequence of our good deeds, while misfortune does not always follow malevolence. This anomaly is highlighted in the aptly named Wisdom literature, especially in the books of Job and Ecclesiastes. As a consequence, Judaeo-Christian thinking began to consider that reward and punishment were not to be found in this life, but rather in the after-life. However, with recent psychological and social scientific research detailing how altruistic actions do indeed have a close relationship with our well-being and happiness, perhaps we can begin to reclaim something of the 'reap what you sow' principle. Evidence suggests, for example, that religious people are generally happier and more fulfilled than those with no faith, due largely to the fact that membership of a faith community involves supportive relationships, social involvement and thinking beyond selfish interests.

In the New Testament, Christ is less concerned with the consequences of our actions on ourselves (although this is certainly not ignored), and more concerned with how our actions impact other people. How we expect to be treated ourselves is posited as a guide to how we treat others. 'In everything, do to others what you would have them do to you,' he urged his disciples (Matt. 7.12). This 'Golden Rule' is, of course, a basic ethical principle that is found in all of the major global religions. Christ, however, maintains that our benevolent deeds should not merely benefit our friends and families. In the parable of the good Samaritan, the hero hails from a racial group hated by first-century Jewish people. Thus, Christ tells us that we should extend our love to *all* people, even our enemies.

Caring for and loving each other, then, is integral to the Christian life. After all, when we serve other people, we are serving God. As

Paul exhorted in Galatians 6.2, 'share each other's troubles and problems, and in this way obey the law of Christ' (NLT). We are not saved by our good deeds, as the sixteenth-century reformers reminded us, but our actions are still important, as the desire to emulate Christ's way of living is part and parcel of our faith. 'Clothe yourselves with compassion, kindness, humility, gentleness and patience,' wrote Paul to the Colossians (3.12).

Such love of neighbour demands our time, resources and emotional involvement. Christ himself is a model for the redemptive suffering that leads us to care for others. Suffering alongside others is, after all, at the heart of the incarnation. This is true 'compassion' – a word William Tyndale invented in the first English Bible. We live, then, as Christ's representatives in the contemporary world, imitating his compassionate, forgiving nature. By doing so, we become 'God in skin', as we take the role of agents of the divine presence to others.

Paradoxically, however, our own imitation and representation of God's character also allows us to recognize God in others. Each one of us is, after all, created in God's image. We represent Christ to those whom we regard to be Christ. 'Christ plays in ten thousand places,' wrote Gerard Manley Hopkins, 'lovely in limbs, lovely in eyes not his.' As such, we encounter Jesus in the most unexpected places and people. Henri Nouwen, on returning from the South American slums, claimed that he recognized the Lord's voice, face and touch in each and every person he met. 'Whatever you do for the least of them,' maintained Christ, 'you do for me' (Matt. 25.40). In the end, even the tomb could not confine Christ's spirit, as it remains among us in those who help us and in those whom we help.

Christians, then, are not called to a life of isolation. Even prominent contemplatives, like the Trappist Thomas Merton, have emphasized the importance of loving and helping others. *The Cloud of Unknowing* asserts that action naturally follows contemplation. When it does, we become, in the words of Mother Teresa, 'pencils in the hand of God'. A number of Christian thinkers, including C. S. Lewis, John Hick and Philip Yancey, have even posited our willingness to help others as one answer to the problem of theodicy. Without the horror of suffering, we would be unable to practise kindness, generosity, unselfishness and agapeic love. Our personality's moral qualities are, indeed, forged through our own suffering and how we react to the suffering of others. In contemplating the compassion shown between the incarcerated of the Second World War camps of the Far East, Ernest Gordon wrote: 'True, there was hatred. But there was also love. There was death. But there was also life. God had not left us. He was with us, calling us to live the divine life in fellowship.' Perhaps service is the natural consequence of such a realization of God's immanence in our pain. By recognizing God's presence in pain, we are led out of our private enclave of suffering to solidarity with all those who suffer.

The practicalities of helping others

The practice of helping others can become the most rewarding of the building blocks we have considered. It can also, however, be the most potentially damaging, both to ourselves and to others. It is, then, imperative, once we decide to give our time and energy as a gift to help others, that we turn towards discernment. Going through a process of deciding where, when and how we offer our help is essential, especially if we are suffering ourselves. At the root of this discernment is awareness – of situations, of others and, most of all, of ourselves.

We all have different gifts and ways of helping, and so sometimes our own particular way will not be suited for certain situations, issues or people. The process of working out when and how our help is useful will often involve taking time and space before responding to an initial feeling or thought. We should ensure that we do not slip into the interfering presumptuousness and unsolicited advice that Job's friends offered. Once we discern whom we will help, our role will simply entail being fully present with our time, talents and resources, and thus being rooted in a shared present moment. As such, we should ensure that we are not listening 'with one ear' or keeping company 'with one eye on the clock'. Our whole being must be present when we help another.

Throughout this process, however, it is important for us not to be hard on ourselves. We must not over-exert ourselves or mask our own suffering through an over-concentration on others. Sometimes, for our own good, we should even abstain from our automatic reflex of helping others, but rather pray silently in the background. An addiction to helpfulness is ultimately damaging to all involved, including ourselves. It is also imperative that we cultivate inner-kindness, alongside our outward displays of kindness. Such an inner-kindness should include compassion towards both others and ourselves. After all, it is difficult to love others, if we first do not love ourselves. 'Love your neighbour *as yourself*,' urged Christ (Matt. 22.39).

If we are not able to cultivate a healthy love of ourselves, then, our generosity to others can merely become a veil for a shortage of self-worth. The more we appreciate and respect ourselves, despite our frailties, the more we will be able to love and respect other people around us, despite theirs. Neither should we engender a self-centred pride or expect credit and praise for any of our efforts. Ego-gratification is not our aim. Our 'acts of random kindness', to use a phrase from the film *Evan Almighty* (2007), are rewards in themselves, as, internally, through them we are reassured that there is hope and meaning to be gleaned in our lives.

Helping others and awareness

Our attitude towards our own painful circumstances seems to lay the foundation for our attitude towards the suffering of others. When we approach our suffering with apathy, denial and suppression, situations are approached exclusively from the perspective of endurance. This can lead to individualism, isolation and a lack of sensitivity for the afflictions of others. As a result, our relationships with others can centre on control, as we, often unconsciously, try to manipulate, coerce, placate, intimidate or flatter. However, if we approach our suffering with awareness and acceptance, we can learn to look outwards in a positive, benevolent way. There is, after all, no better healer than a wounded healer, and, in the process of reaching out to others, we may well find that our own pain will be eased.

Yet, even most books dealing with awareness are 'self-help' books, which, as the name implies, often elevate the self over the corporate. The prevailing individualistic and consumerist attitude of our society certainly makes helping others counter-cultural. We live in a 'me-culture', rather than a 'you-culture'. Still, at a personal, community and national level, we can take opportunities to get involved in numerous ventures. We could help family and friends, or we could give time to strangers. There are, in fact, over half a million community groups in the UK, many of them looking for volunteers. We could, therefore, help out with one of them, with some public service, or with a church project. Not only will this distract us from our own suffering, but it can show us how beautiful life can be, despite deprivation and pain.

As we engage in helping others in their dark hours, then, we are, in some small way, taking creative revenge on our own suffering. Our particular way of helping people need not be grandiose or outwardly impressive. It may, indeed, be very basic – caring for our children, visiting an elderly or sick neighbour, helping a friend in need, feeding a neighbour's pet, or tending an elderly person's garden. Even small actions can make a great difference in people's lives and can have far-reaching consequences, not least in the fact that they create positive memories for the other person, which further blesses them. 'I long to accomplish a great and noble task,' stated Helen Keller, who was struck blind and deaf at an early age, 'but it is my chief duty to accomplish humble tasks as though they were great and noble.'

However brief or seemingly insignificant our compassion, forgiveness, justice and generosity, the divine will be present. As such, our actions enable all parties to glimpse the eternal truth that God loves us more than we could ever conceive. It is, however, also important for us to remember that God is not only present when we help others. He is also present when others help us. Sometimes we simply need to relinquish control and open ourselves to receiving love and compassion from others. As Ecclesiastes reminds us, there is a time for all things – a time for us to love and a time for us to be loved. Thus, we allow others to minister to us and care for us during our own suffering.

None of us is totally independent from each other and so we all need both to be helped by others and to feel that we are helping others. 'The life of an individual,' claimed Albert Einstein, 'has meaning only in so far as it aids in making the life of every living thing nobler and more beautiful.' The world-renowned cellist Pablo Casals described all of us as leaves on the tree of humanity. We all are connected to each other and rely on the whole for sustenance. From the moment of our birth onwards, others do so much for us. We are dependent on them in so many ways. It is, therefore, only natural that we give freely to each other, as others have given to us. To recognize that we are all inter-connected in this manner allows us to see how our own suffering relates to that of others. We are not so different from each other and our afflictions differ only in detail. As such, when one of us suffers, all of us do. As the Russian poet Konstantin Simonov noted, there is 'no sorrow that is alien sorrow'. Thus, *all* suffering should concern *all* of us.

Epilogue: looking ahead

'To be extraordinary means to see things others can't and to suffer things others don't'   *Gin Gwai in* The Eye *(2002)*

'There's more to life than increasing its speed'   *Mahatma Gandhi*

As a timid young teenager, I was not exactly a Casanova. My early history of failed romantic exploits came to a head when I posted a red rose and beautifully composed poem through the door of the wrong house. The octogenarian recipient of my pledge of undying love was rather surprised, to say the least. I was, indeed, a hopeless romantic, but, unfortunately, 'hopeless' was the operative word! My mother tried to soften the embarrassment in a way that served merely to exacerbate the pain. After all, there is only one thing worse than getting no Valentine cards at fifteen years old, and that is getting a solitary one from your own sympathetic mum! In the card, she reassured me that my fortunes would change. The reason for her certainty, she explained, was that I had the one thing that attracted all the women to my dad when he was younger. Was it charm? Or wit? Or looks? Unfortunately not. It was the 'Hughes frown', which apparently, she explained in a completely unbiased way(!), is 'ruggedly attractive'. The males of our family certainly do have a default frown on our brows. Rather than being a blessing in my life, however, this frown has saddled me down the years, being a physical emblem of anxiety and of any suffering I am enduring.

Each one of us is a product of our thoughts and, down the years, each time I've looked in the mirror, my frown has forcefully brought this home to me. As we react to our situations, we create our own little worlds. Each day therefore becomes a battle to keep the burdens of our lives from polluting our minds with oppressive thoughts. Yet, it need not be this way. If our thoughts are hopeful and health-affirming, our worlds can be transformed entirely, whatever the state of our outward circumstances. Through slowing down the pace of my life, in practising awareness and acceptance, I soon noticed that the frown on my face was physically relaxing. Nothing and no one can completely take away the anxiety and stress that accompanies suffering. But through connecting with the transcendent in our lives, the shackles around our minds are loosed and we discover a new freedom and a new peace. As St Paul asserted in his letter to the Philippians, we can learn 'the secret of being content in any and every situation' (4.12).

Yet, the fact remains that until we encounter suffering in our lives, whether our own or that of a loved one, most of us fail to even recognize how imperative it is for us to consider questions of meaning. A recent study of college students in the US showed that, while 70 per cent of them believed that 'wealth' was an essential goal for which to strive, only 40 per cent regarded a meaningful philosophy of life as important. It often takes a period of unhappiness or difficulty for us to get our priorities in order and to find that purpose we so need. As Swedish poet Tomas Tranströmer writes: 'In the middle of the forest is a glade which can only be found by someone who is lost.' Viktor Frankl claims that, if we fail to discover such hope and meaning in the afflictions that we endure, we are doomed. The prisoner in Auschwitz who could not forge meaning from his suffering, for example, 'simply gave up; there he remained, lying in his own excreta, and nothing bothered him any more'.

While it may well be during a period of suffering that we are compelled to face ultimate questions of meaning, our resultant philosophy must be equally applicable in times of joy as it is in times of tribulation. Meaning is, in many ways, personal and unique to each individual. Yet the foundations of awareness and acceptance are a common starting point for all of us to explore where purpose can break through in our lives. When we truly live life in slow motion, our daily existence ceases to be a blur and clarity ensues. The 'building blocks' this book has examined are but five places where we can encounter an actualization of hope. They are, of course, by no means the only places where we can glean significance in our lives. By opening our sense of awareness to signals of transcendence, we may well be surprised by which areas of our lives and the world around us help us to find strength in our weakness and light in our darkness.

Meaning, then, is not to be found through mental or academic activity. It is not even to be discovered through rigid religious practices. Rather, it can be gleaned through our physical experience of other people and the world around us. This is where hope is actualized. This is where the divine speaks and reveals himself. God is, after all, a 'lover of life' (Wisd. 11.26). Jesus himself lived out such an affirmation of existence and he calls us to do the same – to practise the presence of God and recognize the divine imprint in our daily lives.

Thus, we have to look beyond the 'building blocks' themselves to find eternal meaning. We experience God in the physical world in much the same way as we watch a solar eclipse. We do not stare directly at the sun, but instead watch through something on which the amazing spectacle is projected. God's light falls on our world, and through matter, emotions and experiences we can truly experience him. In this way, during our times of trial he does not offer a *supernatural rescue* to us, but he does become a *supernatural resource* for us. As such a healing resource, he serves to strengthen and inspire us as we become more and more aware of his grace, woven in the fabric of our universe.

Through such a positive engagement with life, then, we learn *how* to suffer. While we continue to take the darkness of suffering seriously, we certainly do not need to succumb completely. In time, we learn how to act during our times of pain, rather than react to them. Through doing so, we can reach a place where we recognize how our lives have been shaped and defined by each difficulty and disease that has descended upon us. Our experiences when we suffer therefore become grist for the mill of finding meaning in the seeming meaninglessness of existence. 'Crystal rain falls from black clouds,' asserts an old Persian saying. It is, after all, often our daily struggle that contributes most to our lives. In the film *Rocky Balboa* (2006), the ageing boxer, played by Sylvester Stallone, explains to his son that the world is not all 'sunshine and rainbows'. In fact, life can be 'mean and nasty'. This need not, however, debilitate us completely. The world may, indeed, continually hit us hard and with reckless abandon, but our reaction to the pounding we receive can form and define our character. 'It ain't about how hard you hit back,' he concludes, 'it's about how hard you can get hit and keep moving forward.'

Adversity, then, plays a defining role in our lives. It is ultimately up to us whether it becomes a curse or, paradoxically, a blessing. Our greatest burdens can, indeed, become our greatest gifts. As Emily Dickinson wrote in her poem 'Essential Oils Are Wrung':

> Essential Oils are wrung;
> The Attar from the Rose
> Is not expressed by suns alone,
> It is the gift of screws.

Like diamonds, which sparkle all the more brightly the more facets that are cut, our lives can learn to reflect the light of life all the more brilliantly if we have many cuts. This does not mean we should be masochistically thankful for the suffering in our lives. We can, however, learn to become grateful for the opportunity to respond to our circumstances, to forge good out of bad and life out of death. 'I lay there on rotting prison straw . . .', wrote Alexander Solzhenitsyn of his time in a Soviet gulag, 'I nourished my soul there, and I say without hesitation: Bless you, prison, for having been in my life.'

When we find the courage to face suffering in this way, we experience first hand the power of the resurrection. In forging hope and meaning out of the hopelessness and meaninglessness of affliction, we find that light and life break through darkness and death. Our faith, after all, offers a counter-cultural 'resurrection of the weakest' in response to today's secular 'survival of the fittest' attitude. The psychiatrist Elisabeth Kübler-Ross visited Majdanek concentration camp after its liberation in 1945. There she found countless pictures of butterflies that prisoners had scratched with their fingernails into the walls. Here was the universal emblem of transformation and hope, the butterfly, in the midst of such terrible suffering. Whatever dark chrysalis we find ourselves trapped inside, the promise of new birth, full of colour and vitality, is never far away. We soon find that God has used our seemingly broken lives to carry out his unforeseeable plans. After all, out of the pain and suffering of the cross and the darkness of the wait in the tomb, came the joy and freedom of resurrection. 'Although the world is full of suffering,' concluded Helen Keller, 'it is full also of the overcoming of it.'

Bibliography

The 'general' bibliography below lists texts that have been used as background reading for the book as a whole. A separate bibliography is then included for each chapter. Many of the quotations I have used in this book have been collected over many years from films, music lyrics, books, reliable internet sources and television programmes. Each chapter's bibliography, though, provides a list of the texts that I used for background reading, and also offers readers the opportunity to explore further each topic.

General reading

Robert E. Barron, *The Strangest Way: Walking the Christian Path* (Orbis, New York 2002)

Andrew Bienkowski and Mary Akers, *The Greatest Gift: Lessons Learned From Exile in Siberia* (Pocket, London 2009)

Richard J. Foster and James Bryan Smith (eds), *Devotional Classics: Selected Readings for the Individual and Groups* (Hodder and Stoughton, London 2003)

Viktor E. Frankl, *Man's Search for Meaning: The Classic Tribute to Hope from the Holocaust* (Rider, London 2004)

Richard Harries, *God Outside the Box: Why Spiritual People Object to Christianity* (SPCK, London 2002)

Martin Israel, *Happiness That Lasts* (Cassell, London 1999)

Martin Laird, *Into the Silent Land: A Guide to the Christian Practice of Contemplation* (OUP, Oxford 2006)

Alister McGrath, *Christian Theology: An Introduction* (Blackwell, Oxford 2001)

E. L. Miller and Stanley Grenz, *Introduction to Contemporary Theologies* (Fortress, Minneapolis 1998)

Thomas Moore, *Dark Nights of the Soul: A Guide to Finding Your Way Through Life's Ordeals* (Piatkus, London 2007)

Daniel J. O'Leary, *Travelling Light: Your Journey to Wholeness – A Book of Breathers to Inspire You Along the Way* (Columba, Dublin 2005)

John Ortberg, *When the Game Is Over, It All Goes Back in the Box* (Zondervan, Grand Rapids 2007)

Desmond Tutu, *God Has a Dream: A Vision of Hope for Our Time* (Rider, London 2004)

Martin Warner, *Known to the Senses: Five Days of the Passion* (Continuum, London 2006)

Philip Yancey, *Rumours of Another World: What on Earth Are We Missing?* (Zondervan, Grand Rapids 2004)

Prologue: beyond thinking

Jeffrey Brantley, *Calming Your Anxious Mind: How Mindfulness and Compassion Can Free You from Anxiety, Fear, and Panic* (New Harbinger, Oakland 2007)

Richard Carlson, *Stop Thinking, Start Living: Discover Lifelong Happiness* (Element, London 2003)

Mary Margaret Funk, *Thoughts Matter: The Practice of Spiritual Life* (Continuum, New York 2005)

Mary Margaret Funk, *Tools Matter for Practicing the Spiritual Life* (Continuum, New York 2007)

Julian of Norwich, *Revelations of Divine Love* (D.S. Brewer, Cambridge 1998)

Julian of Norwich, *The Showings of Julian of Norwich*, (ed.) Denise Baker (W.W. Norton, New York 2005)

1 Suffering

Jane Austen, *Mansfield Park* (Penguin, London 2006)

Brian Davies, *The Reality of God and the Problem of Evil* (Continuum, London 2006)

John Donne, *Devotions Upon Emergent Occasions (together with Death's Duel)* (Vintage, New York 1999)

F. Dostoevsky, *The Brothers Karamazov* (Vintage, London 2004)

Donald Eadie, *Grain in Winter: Reflections for Saturday People* (Epworth, Peterborough 2003)

Charles B. Handy, *Waiting for the Mountain to Move: And Other Reflections on Life* (Arrow, London 1995)

Brian Keenan, *An Evil Cradling* (Vintage, London 1993)

Kazoh Kitamori, *Theology of the Pain of God* (SCM, London 1966)

C. S. Lewis, *The Problem of Pain* (Fount, London 2002)

Michael Mayne, *The Enduring Melody* (DLT, London 2007)

A. A. Milne, *House at Pooh Corner* (Egmont, London 2004)

Jürgen Moltmann, *The Crucified God* (SCM, London 1974)

Robert Corin Morris, *Suffering and the Courage of God: Exploring How Grace and Suffering Meet* (Paraclete, Brewster 2005)

Dorothee Soelle, *Suffering* (DLT, London 1975)

Simone Weil, *Gravity and Grace* (Routledge, London 2002)

Holly Whitcomb, *Seven Spiritual Gifts of Waiting* (Augsburg, Minneapolis 2005)

Barry Whitney, *What Are They Saying About God and Evil?* (Paulist, New York 1989)

N. T. Wright, *Evil and the Justice of God* (SPCK, London 2006)

Philip Yancey, *Where Is God When It Hurts?* (Marshall Pickering, London 1998)

2 Foundations: awareness

Mitch Albom, *Tuesdays with Morrie: An Old Man, a Young Man and Life's Greatest Lesson* (Time Warner, London 2006)

Jean-Pierre de Caussade, *Abandonment to Divine Providence* (Image, New York 1975)

Anthony de Mello, *Awareness* (Zondervan, Grand Rapids 1997)

Anthony de Mello, *Sadhana: A Way to God – Christian Exercises in Eastern Form* (Image, New York 1984)

Tilden Edwards, *Living in the Presence: Spiritual Exercises to Open Our Lives to the Awareness of God* (Harper, San Francisco 1995)

James Finley, *Christian Meditation: Experiencing the Presence of God* (Harper, San Francisco 2005)

Richard Foster, *Celebration of Discipline: The Path to Spiritual Growth* (Hodder and Stoughton, London 2005)

James W. Goll, *The Lost Art of Practicing His Presence* (Destiny Image, Shippensburg 2005)

Thich Nhat Hanh, *The Miracle of Mindfulness: A Manual on Meditation* (Rider, London 2008)

Thomas Keating, *Heart of the World: An Introduction to Contemplative Christianity* (Crossroad, New York 1999)

Thomas Keating, *The Better Part: Stages of Contemplative Living* (Continuum, New York 2000)

Brother Lawrence, *The Practice of the Presence of God: Conversations and Letters of Brother Lawrence* (Oneworld, Oxford 2006)

C. S. Lewis, *They Stand Together: The Letters of C. S. Lewis to Arthur Greeves* (Collins, London 1979)

C. S. Lewis, *Surprised by Joy* (Fount, London 1998)

Mary Jo Meadow, Kevin Culligan and Daniel Chowning, *Christian Insight Meditation: Following in the Footsteps of John of the Cross* (Wisdom, Boston 2007)

Michael Meredith, *The Thoughtful Guide to Science and Religion: Using Science, Experience and Religion to Discover Your Own Destiny* (O Books, Winchester 2005)

Thomas Merton, *Contemplative Prayer* (DLT, London 1981)

3 Foundations: acceptance

Richard Adams, *Watership Down* (Penguin, London 1973)

Mitch Albom, *Tuesdays with Morrie: An Old Man, a Young Man and Life's Greatest Lesson* (Time Warner, London 2006)

Jean-Pierre de Caussade, *Abandonment to Divine Providence* (Image, New York 1975)

Michael J. Fox, *Lucky Man* (Ebury, London 2003)

Gerald W. Hughes, 'Foreword', in Michael Mayne, *The Enduring Melody* (DLT, London 2007) (NB the quotation is taken from Hughes's description of Michael Mayne's approach to suffering and is adapted to the second person plural.)

Julian of Norwich, *Revelations of Divine Love* (D.S. Brewer, Cambridge 1998)

Julian of Norwich, *The Showings of Julian of Norwich*, (ed.) Denise Baker (W.W. Norton, New York 2005)

C. S. Lewis, *God in the Dock: Essays on Theology* (Fount, London 1990)

Jacques Lusseyran, *And There Was Light: Autobiography of Jacques Lusseyran, Blind Hero of the French Resistance* (Morning Light, Sandpoint 2006)

Edward Norman, *Out of the Depths: The 'Daily Telegraph' Meditations* (Continuum, London 2001)

Richard Rohr, *Simplicity: The Freedom of Letting Go* (Crossroad, New York 2003)

4 Building blocks: nature

Karen Armstrong, *In the Beginning: A New Reading of Genesis* (Fount, London 1998)

Augustine, *Confessions* (Penguin, London 1961)

Ian C. Bradley, *God Is Green: Ecology for Christianity and the Environment* (DLT, London 1990)

Thomas Browne, *Religio Medici* (CUP, Cambridge 1955)

Elizabeth Barrett Browning, *Aurora Leigh and Other Poems* (Penguin, London 1995)

Bill Bryson, *A Short History of Nearly Everything* (Black Swan, London 2004)

Anne Dillard, *Pilgrim at Tinker Creek* (Harper Perennial, New York 2007)

John Donne, *Devotions Upon Emergent Occasions (together with Death's Duel)* (Vintage, New York 1999)

Hermann Hesse, *Peter Camenzind* (Picador, New York 2003)

Martin J. Hodson and Margot Hodson, *Cherishing the Earth: How to Care for God's Creation* (Monarch, Oxford 2008)

Julian of Norwich, *Revelations of Divine Love* (D.S. Brewer, Cambridge 1998)

Julian of Norwich, *The Showings of Julian of Norwich*, (ed.) Denise Baker (W.W. Norton, New York 2005)

Jon Krakauer, *Into the Wild* (Anchor, New York 1997)

C. S. Lewis, *They Stand Together: The Letters of C. S. Lewis to Arthur Greeves* (Collins, London 1979)

C. S. Lewis, *Miracles* (Fount, London 2002)

Robert MacFarlane, *The Wild Places* (Granta, London 2007)

Alister E. McGrath, *Science and Religion: An Introduction* (Blackwell, Oxford 1999)

Lewis Regenstein, *Replenish the Earth: A History of Organized Religions' Treatment of Animals and Nature – Including Bible's Message of Conservation and Kindness toward Animals* (SCM, London 1991)

Dylan Thomas, *Under Milk Wood* (Penguin, London 2000)

R. S. Thomas, *The Collected Poems 1945–1990* (Phoenix, London 2004)

Henry David Thoreau, *Walden; or Life in the Woods* (Dover, New York 1995)

5 Building blocks: laughter

Henri Bergson, *Laughter: An Essay on the Meaning of the Comic* (MacMillan, New York 1913)

Jacqueline Bussie, *Ethical and Theological Resistance in Wiesel, Morrison, and Endo* (T&T Clark, London 2007)

Jimmy Carr and Lucy Greeves, *The Naked Jape: Uncovering the Hidden World of Jokes* (Penguin, London 2007)

Deepak Chopra, *Why Is God Laughing?: The Path to Joy and Spiritual Optimism* (Harmony, New York 2008)

Christopher Coelho, *A New Kind of Fool: Meditations on St Francis* (Burns and Oates, Tunbridge Wells 1991)

Harvey Cox, *The Feast of Fools* (Harvard University Press, Harvard 1969)

Dante, *The Divine Comedy* (OUP, Oxford 2008)

Umberto Eco, *The Name of the Rose* (Vintage, London 1998)

Giles Fraser, *Christianity with Attitude* (Canterbury Press, London 2007)

Graeme Garrett, 'My Brother Esau is an Hairy Man: An Encounter between the Comedian and Preacher', in *Scottish Journal of Theology*, Vol. 33

Allen Klein, *The Healing Power of Humour* (Tarcher/Putnam, New York 1989)

Karl-Josef Kuschel, *Laughter: A Theological Reflection* (SCM, London 1994)

Reinhold Neibuhr, 'Humour and Faith' in *Holy Laughter* (ed.) Conrad Hyers (Seaberry Press, New York 1969)

F. W. Nietzsche, *First Spoke Zarathustra* (Penguin, London 2003)

Barry Sanders, *Sudden Glory: Laughter as Subversive History* (Beacon, Boston 1995)

M. A. Screech, *Laughter at the Foot of the Cross* (Penguin, London 1999)

Phil Simmons, *Learning to Fall: The Blessings of an Imperfect Life* (Bantam, New York 2002)

6 Building blocks: memory

J. M. Barrie, *Courage: A Rectorial Address 1922* (Kessinger, Whitefish 2005)

Bill Bryson, *A Short History of Nearly Everything* (Black Swan, London 2004)

Albert Camus, *The Outsider* (Penguin, London 2006)

Gregory Dix, *The Shape of the Liturgy* (Continuum, London 2005)

Charles Elliott, *Memory and Salvation* (DLT, London 1995)

William Faulkner, *Intruder in the Dust* (Vintage, London 1996)

Kathleen Fischer, *Imaging Life after Death: Love That Moves the Sun and Stars* (Paulist, New York 2004)

Giles Fraser, *Christianity with Attitude* (Canterbury Press, London 2007)

Grey Gowrie, *Third Day: New and Selected Poems* (Carcanet, Manchester 2008)

Doris Grumbach *The Pleasure of their Company* (Beacon, Boston 2000)

Gary Hayden and Michael Picard, *This Book Does Not Exist: Adventures in the Paradoxical* (Continuum, London 2009)

Brian Keenan, *An Evil Cradling* (Vintage, London 1993)

James Laird, *Feelings: The Perception of Self* (OUP, Oxford 2007)

C. S. Lewis, *Surprised by Joy* (Fount, London 1998)

C. S. Lewis, *Weight of Glory: And Other Addresses* (Zondervan, Grand Rapids 2001)

C. Robert Mesle, *Process Theology: A Basic Introduction* (Chalice, St Louis 1993)

John Polkinghorne, *The Faith of a Physicist* (Augsburg Fortress, Minneapolis 1996)

Macrina Wiederkehr, *Gold in Your Memories: Sacred Moments, Glimpses of God* (Ave Maria, Notre Dame 2000)

7 Building blocks: art

Diane Apostolos-Cappadona (ed.), *Art, Creativity and the Sacred: Anthology in Religion and Art* (Contiuum, New York 1998)

Jeff Astley, Timothy Hone and Mark Savage (eds), *Creative Chords: Studies in Music, Theology and Christian Formation* (Gracewing, Leominster 2000)

Nick Cave, 'Introduction', in *The Gospel According to Mark* (Canongate, Edinburgh 1998)

Nick Cave, 'Introduction: The Secret Life of the Love Song', in *The Complete Lyrics 1978–2001* (Penguin, London 2001)

Michael Paul Gallagher, *Dive Deeper: The Human Poetry of Faith* (DLT, London 2001)

Anne Lamott, *Bird by Bird: Some Instructions on Writing and Life* (Anchor, New York 1995)

Gordon Lynch, *After Religion: Generation X and the Search for Meaning* (DLT, London 2002)

Michael Mayne, *The Enduring Melody* (DLT, London 2007)

Ian McEwan, *Atonement* (Vintage, London 2001)

Shaun McNiff, *Art Heals: How Creativity Cures the Soul* (Shambhala, Boston 2004)

Bel Mooney (ed.), *Devout Sceptics: Conversations on Faith and Doubt* (Hodder and Stoughton, London 2004)

Stephen Pinker, *The Blank Slate: The Modern Denial of Human Nature* (Penguin, London 2003)

Oliver Sacks, *Musicophilia: Tales of Music and the Brain* (Picador, London 2008)

Franky Schaeffer, *Addicted to Mediocrity: 20th Century Christians and the Arts* (Crossway, Wheaton 1993)

Steve Turner, *Imagine: A Vision for Christians and the Arts* (Inter Varsity, Downers Grove 2001)

Donald C. Whittle, *Christianity and the Arts* (Mowbray, London 1966)

Macrina Wiederkehr, *Gold in Your Memories: Sacred Moments, Glimpses of God* (Ave Maria, Notre Dame 2000)

Philip Yancey, *Where Is God When It Hurts?* (Marshall Pickering, London 1998)

8 Building blocks: helping others

Mitch Albom, *Tuesdays with Morrie: An Old Man, a Young Man and Life's Greatest Lesson* (Time Warner, London 2006)

Nick Baylis, *The Rough Guide to Happiness* (Rough Guides, London 2009)

The Cloud of Unknowing (Paulist Press, New York 1981)

Stefan Einhorn, *The Art of Being Kind* (Sphere, London 2008)

George Eliot, *Adam Bede* (Penguin, London 2008)

E. M. Forster, *A Passage to India* (Penguin, London 2005)

Ernest Gordon, *To End All Wars: A True Story About the Will to Survive and the Courage to Forgive* (Zondervan, Grand Rapids 2002)

John Hick, *Evil and the Love of God* (Palgrave Macmillan, Basingstoke 2007)

Lewis Hyde, *The Gift: How the Creative Spirit Transforms the World* (Canongate, Edinburgh 2007)

Helen Keller, *The Story of My Life* (Dover, New York 1997)

Richard Layard, *Happiness: Lessons from a New Science* (Penguin, London 2006)

C. S. Lewis, *The Problem of Pain* (Fount, London 2002)

Paul Martin, *Making Happy People: The Nature of Happiness and Its Origins in Childhood* (Harper Perennial, London 2006)

Gerald G. May, *The Awakened Heart: Opening Yourself to the Love You Need* (Harper, San Francisco 1993)